All About Trees

Created and designed by
the editorial staff of
ORTHO BOOKS

Project Editors
Nancy Arbuckle
Cedric Crocker

Illustrators
Ron Hildebrand
Frank Hildebrand
Rick van Genderen

Designer
Gary Hespenheide

Ortho Books

Publisher
Richard E. Pile, Jr.

Editorial Director
Christine Jordan

Production Director
Ernie S. Tasaki

Managing Editors
Robert J. Beckstrom
Michael D. Smith
Sally W. Smith

System Manager
Linda M. Bouchard

Marketing Specialist
Daniel Stage

Sales Manager
Thomas J. Leahy

Distribution Specialist
Barbara F. Steadham

Technical Consultant
J. A. Crozier, Jr., Ph.D.

Address all inquiries to:
Ortho Books
Chevron Chemical Company
Consumer Products Division
Box 5047
San Ramon, CA 94583

Copyright © 1982, 1992
Chevron Chemical Company
All rights reserved under international and Pan-American copyright conventions.

2 3 4 5 6 7 8 9
93 94 95 96 97

ISBN 0-89721-248-7
Library of Congress Catalog Card Number 92-70589

Chevron Chemical Company
6001 Bollinger Canyon Road
San Ramon, CA 94583

Writers
Monica Brandies; Brandon, Fla.
Franklin J. Chan, Arborist, City of Sacramento; Sacramento, Calif.
Francis Ching, Director, Los Angeles County Botanical Garden and Arboretum; Arcadia, Calif.
William Collins, American Garden-Cole Nursery; Circleville, Ohio
Morgan "Bill" Evans, Landscape Architect; Malibu, Calif.
William Flemer III, Princeton Nurseries; Princeton, N.J.
John Ford, Curator, Secrest Arboretum; Wooster, Ohio
Fred Galle, Curator, Callaway Gardens; Pine Mountain, Ga.
Richard W. Harris, Professor of Landscape Horticulture, University of California; Davis, Calif.
Raymond P. Korbobo, Landscape Design, Rutgers University; New Brunswick, N.J.
Fred Lang, Landscape Architect; South Laguna, Calif.
Frank G. Mackaness, J. Frank Schmidt & Son Co., wholesale nursery; Boring, Oreg.
Brian O. Mulligan, University of Washington Arboretum; Seattle, Wash.
Robert L. Ticknor, Professor of Horticulture, Oregon State University; Aurora, Oreg.

Photography Editor
Roberta Spieckerman

Special Thanks to
Catherine Habiger; Menlo Park, Calif.
Karen Heilman; San Francisco, Calif.
Bridget Makk; Menlo Park, Calif.
Paul Meyer; Chestnut Hill, Pa.
Orchard Nursery; Lafayette, Calif.

Copy Chief
Melinda E. Levine

Editorial Coordinator
Cass Dempsey

Copyeditor
Rebecca Pepper

Proofreader
Deborah Bruner

Indexer
Elinor Lindheimer

Layout & Composition by
Nancy Patton Wilson

Editorial Assistant
Laurie A. Steele

Associate Editor
Sara Shopkow

Production by
Studio 165

Separations by
Color Tech Corp.

Lithographed in the USA by
Webcrafters, Inc.

Consultants
Robert G. Askew, North Dakota State University; Fargo, N.Dak.
Maggie Baylis; San Francisco, Calif.
Russell B. Beatty, Professor of Landscape Architecture, University of California; Berkeley, Calif.
Bartow H. Bridges, Jr.; Virginia Beach, Va.
L. C. Chadwick, Professor Emeritus, Ohio State University; Columbus, Ohio
John Copeland; Norfolk, Vir.
Robert Cowden; Walnut Creek, Calif.
Francis H. Dean; Newport Beach, Calif.
Dr. James Foret, Dean, College of Agriculture, University of Southwestern Louisiana; Lafayette, La.
William Gould, Professor of Landscape Architecture, University of Maryland; College Park, Md.
Francis R. Gouin, Associate Professor Ornamental Horticulture, University of Maryland; College Park, Md.
Richard Hildreth, Director, State Arboretum; Salt Lake City, Utah
Roger R. Huff; Virginia Beach, Va.
John Kissida, Professor of Landscape Architecture, University of Maryland; College Park, Md.
Andrew Leiser, Professor of Environmental Horticulture, University of California; Davis, Calif.
Clarence E. Lewis, Professor Emeritus, Michigan State University; East Lansing, Mich.
Frederick McGourty; Norfolk, Conn.
Paul W. Meyer, Curator, Morris Arboretum; Chestnut Hill, Pa.
Dr. Henry P. Orr, Professor of Ornamental Horticulture, Auburn University; Auburn, Ala.
Dr. Roland E. Roberts, Texas A & M University; Lubbock, Tex.
Warren Roberts, University Arboretum, University of California; Davis, Calif.
Dr. Arvil Stark; Salt Lake City, Utah
Richard K. Sutton, Assistant Professor of Horticulture, University of Nebraska; Lincoln, Nebr.
Dr. Carl E. Whitcomb, Associate Professor of Horticulture, Oklahoma State University; Stillwater, Okla.
Joseph A. Witt, University of Washington Arboretum; Seattle, Wash.

ORTHENE is a registered trademark of Chevron Chemical Company. SEVIN is a registered trademark of Rhône-Poulenc.

Photographers
Names of photographers are followed by the page numbers on which their work appears. R=right, C=center, L=left, T=top, B=bottom.

William Aplin: 62L, 66R, 72L, 73BR, 76R, 89R, 104L, 107L
Liz Ball: 70L
Laurie Black: 26T, 56T, 73L, 84R, 87R
John Blaustein: 59L
A. Boger: 37L
Charles Callister, Jr.: front cover
Clyde Childress: 100C
Josephine Coatsworth: 101L
S. Collman: 37R
Crandall & Crandall: 11, 22, 46B, 65L, 74R, 78R, 79L, 88R, 97R, 99L, 99C, 101C, 107R
Thomas Eltzroth: 39BL, 39TR, 46T, 57C, 64R, 65R, 66L, 74L, 79R, 80R, 81C, 91L, 91R, 93L, 93R, 95C, 105R
Derek Fell: 8, 10, 16TR, 26B, 38B, 42, 45T, 49, 50B, 51L, 52, 64L, 67L, 67R, 68R, 69L, 69R, 70L, 71R, 79C, 81R, 82L, 83R, 84C, 86C, 90L, 90R, 92L, 98L, 99R, 100L, 101C, 103L, 103R, 104R, 106L, 106R, back cover TL
Saxon Holt: title page, 9B, 12–13, 16TL, 16B, 19T, 25, 27T, 27B, 43, 44B, 47R, 48T, 50T, 51R, 56B, 57R, 62R, 66C, 71L, 72C, 72R, 75L, 78L, 84L, 89L, 91C, 94L, 94R, 98C, back cover BL and R
Jerry Howard/Positive Images: 4–5, 7, 9T, 40–41, 54–55, 97L
Susan Lammers: 90C
Michael Landis: 58L, 76L, 77L, 95R
Michael McKinley: 38T, 47L, 57L, 60L, 68L, 75R, 77R, 86L, 86R, 87L, 100R, 101R
Paul W. Meyer: 6, 39BR, 61R, 63R, 73TR, 78C, 94C, 98R, 102R
Scott Millard: 92R
Ortho Information Services: 53R, 60C, 63L, 80L, 82R, 83L, 85L, 85R, 88L, 95L, 96L, 102L
Pam Peirce: 44T, 45B, 48B, 81L, back cover TR
Susan Roth: 53L
Michael D. Smith: 38C, 39TL, 61L
Wolf von dem Bussche: 58R, 59R, 60R, 77C, 96R, 105L

Front Cover
The unusually shaped leaves of the tulip tree emerge yellowish green in the spring.

Back Cover
Top left: The trunk of a paper birch tree provides a pleasing contrast against a green lawn.
Top right: Japanese black pine is tolerant of salt spray, making it especially useful along the seacoast.
Bottom left: The atlas cedar is a popular blue-foliaged conifer.
Bottom right: The fan-shaped leaves of the maidenhair tree turn a brilliant yellow in the fall.

Title Page
Stately Douglas fir trees surround this beautiful garden.

All About Trees

The World of Trees

Trees provide shade, a natural setting for a home, and walls and ceiling for outdoor living areas. Trees enhance a garden, soften the lines of a building, give a neighborhood character, and add color to the skyline.

Trees serve many purposes, both aesthetic and practical. They can absorb noise, filter the air, and frame attractive views or screen unattractive ones. When used along neighborhood streets, trees provide structural continuity, establishing pleasant connections between houses. They also often enhance property values. Trees can beautify and add grace to otherwise unattractive areas; they can positively affect the quality of life of those who live and work in their midst. Some trees also produce fruit or nuts that can be an important source of food.

Today there is renewed interest in trees. Their importance environmentally as well as aesthetically is now widely discussed. Only small tracts of undisturbed old-growth forest are left in the United States and southern Canada. A growing awareness of the significance of forest land has accompanied its rapid disappearance.

Urbanization and agriculture have taken their toll on land that was once heavily wooded. In rural areas trees were once considered a necessity. Although one might still see clusters of trees marking the site of old homesteads or fence lines, trees that once provided rural homes and farm animals with shade and protection from the wind are fast disappearing. Wooded areas are shrinking as farmers are forced to get every square yard of production from their land. In and around urban areas, trees are being cleared to make way for development and to supply the needs of a growing population.

The beautiful and profuse blossoms of the flowering dogwood stand out brightly against the deep green of this garden.

Although once a common sight, wooded farmyards are now a rarity in many parts of the country. Here, sugar maples show their fall splendor.

As people and buildings become more crowded, the need for greenbelts and the sight of something beautiful and growing to refresh the spirit is more apparent. One aim of this book is to encourage the preservation and increased planting of trees. When chosen carefully and cared for properly, trees will grow and thrive for many years.

TREES AND PEOPLE

In many cities, for many years, there have been ordinances about the kinds of trees that homeowners, landscapers, and city planners can plant. Height restrictions are placed on trees to be planted near utility wires. Trees that are considered messy because they drop fruit, leaves, seeds, or bark may not be planted in heavily used areas. Weak-wooded trees are not allowed along streets or sidewalks, and pollen producers are often prohibited due to the allergic reactions they cause. Because of their invasive root systems that may block or impede drainage, poplars and willows cannot be planted near water pipes or septic systems.

In spite of these restrictions, more and more people have come to appreciate the benefits that trees provide. Trees can be used to shade the large expanses of concrete and pavement that tend to make cities hotter in summer. In a home garden, a few well-chosen and well-placed trees around a house can cut home air-conditioning costs substantially. Evergreens planted on the north and west sides to break the winter wind will also save energy by reducing heating costs. As more and more people appreciate the value and usefulness of trees, local ordinances are being passed to protect existing trees from damage or removal and to encourage the planting of new trees.

Cleaning the Air

The importance of trees for air purification is now recognized and has become more critical as pollution by traffic and industry increases. The proportion of carbon dioxide in the atmosphere is rising at an ever-increasing rate due to the heavy consumption of fossil fuels (oil, coal, and gas) worldwide. The presence of excess carbon dioxide in the atmosphere prevents heat from escaping into space, trapping it inside the earth's atmosphere. This is commonly called the greenhouse effect. Trees purify the air by consuming carbon dioxide and giving off oxygen. Trees represent the oldest, cheapest, and most efficient way of offsetting the current overload of atmospheric carbon dioxide, thus reducing the escalating concern about global warming.

Preserving Trees

At the same time that the need for trees to reduce carbon dioxide in the atmosphere is increasing, trees in urban locations are being threatened by this same pollution. Trees are also being threatened by the encroachment of paving over their root zones, by soil compaction from nearby development, and by drought and other environmental changes. Even as the need for them has grown, trees have become more vulnerable.

Many cities have begun to inventory and preserve their large and valuable trees and to encourage the planting of new ones. Some city governments provide consultants to evaluate city trees as well as those on private property. These consultants can identify the trees that should be kept or those weak ones that should be removed and replaced. They can also advise developers and city officials on how they can adjust construction practices and plans to protect mature trees. Many city arborists and park commissioners are more than willing to suggest appropriate street trees, and in some cases they will help to maintain such trees. Where a service sponsored by the community is not available, homeowners fortunate enough to have mature trees on their property should hire an arborist or tree professional before doing any construction. See page 36 for information on how to choose a qualified tree expert.

Planting Trees

Careful selection is a key factor in the longevity and beauty of trees. Many trees planted in place of those lost have also perished due to repeated errors in selection or care. Because in some urban areas only about one in four newly planted trees will live to maturity, it is not enough to plant a tree for every one that is lost.

Trees represent an investment—in purchase price, maintenance costs, and time. Once planted and nurtured to maturity, a long-lived and much-admired tree that provides beauty, shelter, and comfort for many generations can be considered priceless.

Choose hardy, strong-wooded, nonallergenic species that do not require heavy maintenance (for example, those that do not drop fruit and leaves) and that are well adapted to the local climate and microclimate (see page 42).

Plant trees to fit existing conditions. Where there are narrow planting strips, choose trees whose root systems can accommodate such constraints. Consider the presence of overhead wires and the proximity of patios, walkways, and buildings.

Even within a given species, there will be variation in hardiness or cold tolerance, ability to withstand periods of drought, tolerance of street salting, and responses to other conditions. Some trees are more susceptible to disease or pest problems than others. In selecting trees, consider the potentially devastating consequences of, for example, Dutch elm disease, chestnut blight, or other diseases. When chosen carefully, trees will provide greenery, climate control, and a sense of shelter and security for many years.

Trees are a welcome sight on a city street. These apartment buildings are softened and shaded by redbud growing nearby.

Tree Appreciation—
A Checklist

Concern for trees can sometimes shrink in importance when considered in relation to other world problems. But this is one area where an individual can make a significant impact. Tree planting and care offer opportunities to improve the environment and represent an important contribution to the future. The beauty and pleasure of trees will also bring almost immediate improvements to the yard or garden, increase property values, and enhance the comfort and elegance of our surroundings. Here are a few suggestions for what you can do.

Learn to identify and understand your trees   This may take several seasons, but will make you better able to provide proper care for your trees. A tree may manifest different characteristics depending on climatic variations. For example, some of the finest flowering trees (such as dogwood) may skip a blooming cycle after cold winters in marginal zones. Immediate evaluations of a tree's worth can be inaccurate and misleading. See the "Encyclopedia of Trees" beginning on page 55 for details on the characteristics and needs of individual species.

Many trees change with the seasons by blossoming or shedding leaves. The saucer magnolia is at its best in spring, when it is covered with pink flowers.

Protect trees   Avoid damaging a tree's bark with lawn mowers, nylon-string trimmers, or other gardening tools and practices. Take necessary precautions to protect root systems when building near trees (see page 35). Monitor leaves, limbs, and trunk carefully to detect and prevent or treat pest or disease problems before they become serious.

Remove only weedy or short-lived trees   Preserve large trees as long as practical. Replace trees that are susceptible to disease or that have limited life spans with hardy, adapted species. If choice mature trees suffer damage, seek repair first, with removal only as a last resort.

Prune carefully   Prune trees only when necessary. Although pruning can help restore vigor to a tree and improve its appearance, removing substantial amounts of healthy growth can have an adverse effect. When done properly, pruning can open views and allow more light through while preserving the beauty and health of the tree. See pages 25 to 32 for correct pruning techniques.

Plant as many new trees as can be accommodated   Plan first and select carefully, considering the effect to be achieved, the mature size of trees, and the required maintenance. Plant a few extra trees for shade and screening or to ensure against possible loss.

Care for young trees   Newly planted trees require two to three years for their root systems to become fully established. During this time extra watering and special care are necessary. See pages 19 to 25 for specific information on tree care.

Teach by example   Your concern for trees will motivate your children and anyone else you might influence to value, care for, and appreciate trees. Encourage neighbors and friends to learn about and care for the trees around them.

Appreciate seasonal change   Trees are fascinating to study. They offer unending enjoyment, but require familiarity and close observation to be fully appreciated. Watch deciduous trees for spring blossoms, summer

Top: Although leafless, a grove of white birch will retain its grace and beauty throughout the winter.
Bottom: Only a fraction of the magnificent coast redwoods native to California and Oregon remain.

fruit, fall colors, and the silhouette of their bare branches against the winter sky. Admire evergreens for their constancy, their year-round color, and the way they look with snow on their boughs. By knowing the characteristics and patterns of various trees, you can anticipate and admire their striking show.

Give trees on special occasions Trees make wonderful gifts and are especially appreciated as memorials of births, birthdays, weddings, special holidays, and departed friends. They can be planted in parks, on school or church grounds, in front of public buildings such as libraries and city halls, and in botanical gardens. A small plaque bearing appropriate information adds to their significance. A few years of care can start a living monument.

TREES AND THE WORLD

Many people take trees for granted. Some even consider them nuisances because of the care they require and the chores they create, a problem often made worse by poor tree selection. For centuries there seemed to be so many trees that the very thought of a shortage was inconceivable. Unfortunately, the abuse and devastation of nature's once rich gift of trees and forests has not been reversed by the recent beginning of human understanding and appreciation: It continues to this day.

Our heritage of forests—even the giant redwoods of the Pacific Coast—is perishing. Large portions of the virgin forests in the United States and other industrialized countries have

Tropical rain forests contain thousands of species of plants and animals, many of which are lost as the forests are cleared. Tree ferns like those shown here thrive in the rain forest environment.

been logged, and tropical rain forests are now being lost to agricultural conversion at a tremendous rate. At the same time, there is increasing evidence that the loss of forests may lead to climatic disruptions and global warming that could change our lives drastically.

Fortunately, people are finally realizing the importance of trees to our global welfare. Individuals, groups, and large organizations have begun to work for tree preservation and reforestation to prevent further environmental degradation and climatic change.

Tree Preservation—A Checklist

Awakening public awareness is the key to the preservation of forest land, old growth, and rain forests. As people come to realize that they are only one of many species that inhabit and rely on the earth, progress can be made. The pace of change can be increased considerably

and problems can be solved when people reach beyond their daily lives and try to influence what is happening in the rest of the world. The following are some things that you can do to encourage and ensure the preservation of trees and forest land.

Vote Research the records and positions of elected representatives on issues of reforestation and tree preservation and write to them to express your views. Vote for concerned and productive representatives.

Organize your family, your neighborhood, your church, or your club Groups such as these can play a major role in tree-planting projects or in the care of existing but neglected trees. Most towns and cities in the United States have space around homes and office buildings for additional trees. More tree planting in urban areas could be highly effective in mitigating air-quality problems and reducing carbon dioxide.

Support national and international organizations Conservation and environmental organizations—along with botanical gardens, nature sanctuaries, and arboretums—serve to promote the care and preservation of trees and forests. Some engage in tree care research, have public education programs, and lobby for conservation legislation.

Check the source of fast-food hamburgers Tropical forests are being cleared at an alarming rate to make pasture land for cattle. More than half of Central America's arable land now produces beef, much of it exported to supply various fast-food chains. Much of this land is particularly unsuited for cattle farming. To create it, many square miles of forest are cleared and destroyed. The removal of forest cover leads to soil erosion, and much of the pasture becomes useless after a few years. The process of clearing then begins again, further encroaching on the lands of small farmers and denuding vast tracts of what was once a vital ecosystem. A reduction in the demand for beef from the tropical sources used by fast-food operations could slow or reverse this process.

HOW TO USE THIS BOOK

It takes many lifetimes to learn and large libraries to contain the present body of knowledge about trees, and new information is being discovered all the time. The purpose of this book is to provide gardeners and tree lovers with the information they need to select, plant, maintain, and preserve trees.

The following chapter contains information on buying trees, including appropriate size, root quality, and foliage considerations. Following that is a section on site preparation and planting. Information on watering and feeding, mulching, and pruning follow. Other aspects of tree care and maintenance are also covered, including descriptions of a variety of tree pests and diseases and how to treat them. Review the chapter titles, the photographs, and the index to find the instructions you need for any aspect of tree care.

When large problems on mature trees require the help, equipment, or advice of a tree professional, this chapter also tells how to

find one and how to understand the work that will be done.

The third chapter, a guide for selecting trees, provides lists of trees suited to particular needs. Use it to choose appropriate trees to meet specific conditions. If you need a tree that is tolerant of city conditions, seashore wind and salt spray, or flooding, you will find many possibilities listed in this chapter. Here also are lists of trees notable for their fall color or their winter silhouette. Many other lists are included—see page 43 for the complete chapter contents.

Use the fourth chapter, "Encyclopedia of Trees," to identify trees in your yard and neighborhood and to learn what to expect of them in the changing seasons and the coming years. Use it also when deciding what tree to plant in what spot. Cold tolerance (hardiness) is given for each species. Check for appropriateness to your climate by comparing the climate zone information for each species to the map on page 108.

Information on how tall and wide a particular tree will grow is also given for each species, to help you in selecting and placing young trees. Trees will not develop their full shape unless they have ample room to spread. Which trees give dense shade, which open shade? When will a species bloom? What color will it be? How will it blend with other plantings? What fruit or berries will it produce? What problems might it have? Refer to the species descriptions to find those that will fulfill your needs.

Among the countless species and varieties of trees are ones suited to any yard or garden.

Planting and Care

Trees are complex organisms whose many parts function together so that the tree can grow and thrive. Understanding how the parts of a tree work together will aid you in selecting, planting, and caring for trees.

A protective layer of bark covers the trunk of a tree. Beneath this outer layer of bark is the inner bark (phloem) that is part of the tree's vascular system, carrying nutrients to where they are needed. Between the inner bark and the sapwood is a thin layer called the cambium that produces the new cells for both. Growth in the diameter of a tree's trunk is by cell division and expansion from this thin cylinder of cambium cells. The inner sapwood, or xylem, carries nutrients and water from the roots to the leaves. Beneath the sapwood is the heartwood, an inactive region of sapwood. Heartwood gives the tree strength and rigidity and serves as a depository for stored food and wastes.

The root system of a tree can be quite extensive, depending on the depth and texture of the soil in which it grows. As a tree matures, relatively shallow horizontal roots develop and predominate. Lateral roots form at the base of the trunk and spread to build an extensive network that anchors the tree. Lateral roots also store food. Feeder roots grow from the lateral roots and transport water and nutrients absorbed by the root hairs (microscopic appendages to feeder roots). Root caps produce a continuous supply of new cells that are sloughed off and serve to lubricate the advance of the growing root tip through the soil.

The deodar cedar is considered by many to be the most graceful and refined of the cedars.

The Parts of a Tree

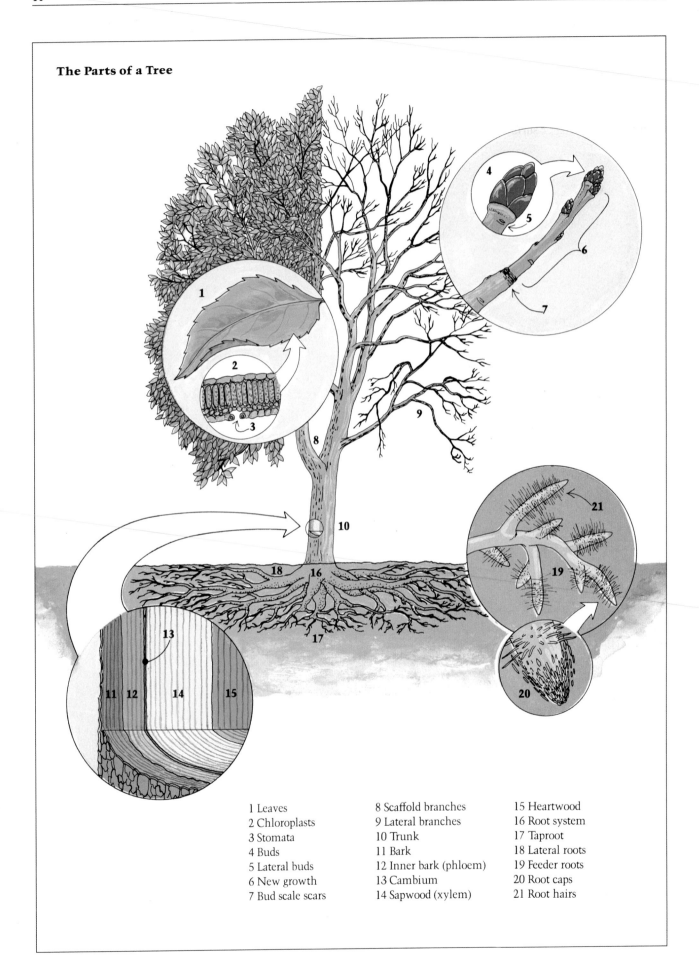

1 Leaves
2 Chloroplasts
3 Stomata
4 Buds
5 Lateral buds
6 New growth
7 Bud scale scars

8 Scaffold branches
9 Lateral branches
10 Trunk
11 Bark
12 Inner bark (phloem)
13 Cambium
14 Sapwood (xylem)

15 Heartwood
16 Root system
17 Taproot
18 Lateral roots
19 Feeder roots
20 Root caps
21 Root hairs

Leaves produce food for the tree and release water and oxygen into the atmosphere. Within leaves, chloroplasts—chlorophyll bodies in which photosynthesis takes place—create food for the tree. Chloroplasts give leaves their green color. On the outer surface of tree leaves are specialized "breathing pores" called stomata through which carbon dioxide enters the tree and water and oxygen are released.

Scaffold branches are the large limbs that give a tree its basic shape. Laterals are secondary branches—mainly horizontal—that create the tree's outline. The leader is the tree's central and primary shoot or branch.

Terminal buds are at the ends of shoots, and lateral buds are along the sides of shoots. These buds contain the undeveloped shoots, leaves, and flowers for the next growing season. If the terminal bud is removed, one or more lateral buds will grow to take its place. Flower buds contain the embryonic reproductive system of the tree.

TREE DEVELOPMENT

Branch growth and development starts at the tip of each shoot, in an area of tissue no larger than a pinpoint. Here, leaves, flowers, and the support and conductive elements of the tree begin. This region and that of the most active stem growth are within the top 1 to 2 inches of the stem.

Growth Patterns

A tree's growth in height takes place through shoots or buds that develop into branches. Shoot growth in some trees lasts for only three to four weeks in spring. For others, it occurs in flushes (periods of growth) during the growing season, while on still others it occurs almost continuously when conditions are favorable. The growth of trees that have a single flush is largely determined by the number of shoots formed in each bud the previous year. On these trees, shoot responses to cultivation—fertilization, for example—will not show up until the following year. Annual shoot growth is one measure of tree vigor and is easy to see on trees that have just one annual flush.

For shoots to grow upright, plants have developed the ability—called heliotropism—to grow toward the sun and away from the pull of gravity. To hold their ever-lengthening shoots

upright, trees and shrubs form an increasing number of stiffer woody cells.

Like shoot growth, the amount of trunk growth differs from species to species and varies according to climate conditions. A tree's growth pattern can be seen in successive growth rings. Wood formed in the spring has larger cells than wood formed later in the year, and wet and dry years are shown in the varying width of growth rings. In general, the width of the annual rings indicates the vigor of a tree in past years.

In most trees used for streets, patios, and landscapes, a strong, upright trunk is desired. Lateral branches encourage the trunk's growth in girth. Horizontal lateral limbs are slow growing. In contrast, upright shoots are more vigorous and are likely to compete with the leader.

Light

Tree growth is influenced not only by wind and gravity, but also by light. Light has much to do with the direction of shoot growth and tree form. Almost everyone is familiar with shoot tips growing toward light, especially with houseplants. The tips of tree shoots react similarly.

Light also plays a part in tree form when trees grow close to one another, particularly if the trees are different species or sizes. The branches growing toward a taller or more dominant tree will not grow as much as those on the more open side of the tree. In time, such a tree will appear to be growing away from the other tree. This may not be noticed unless the more dominant tree is removed. However, give trees enough room to develop their characteristic forms.

TREE SELECTION

Read through this chapter before buying a tree—understanding how to plant a tree and care for it will make the selection process much easier. Trees are most often available for purchase in one of three forms—bare root, balled and burlapped, or container grown. Each of these have different characteristics and varying planting procedures.

Select a medium-sized tree. The biggest of the bunch will not necessarily grow the best. Once planted, a tree of moderate size is likely to reestablish itself more quickly and often will catch up with and surpass a larger tree.

Left: Bare-root trees are grown in fields, dug, and handled with little or no soil on the roots.
Right: Field-grown trees dug with soil around the roots and wrapped in burlap are available for planting the year around.

Bare-Root Trees

Many field-grown, deciduous trees are under-cut, dug, and handled with little or no soil on the roots; hence the term *bare root*. Bare-root trees are dug in late fall and stored so that their roots are kept moist and their tips are dormant. Bare-root trees must be planted while still dormant, and careful handling to avoid root damage is critical.

In large field-grown trees, much of the root mass is cut and left in the field when the trees are dug. Due to the lower root-to-top ratio in these trees, after planting the tops must be lightly thinned so that the roots can supply enough water (particularly in warm weather) to support new leaf growth. Experts recommend thinning limbs rather than a hard pruning of the entire top. Overpruning reduces food reserves held in the twigs; in addition, it limits the photosynthetic capacity of the newly planted tree, thereby inhibiting the formation of new roots.

Check the roots carefully before planting a container-grown tree.

Balled-and-Burlapped Trees

Most field-grown evergreen trees are dug with soil around the roots. The soil ball is wrapped in burlap, hence the term *balled and bur-lapped,* or *B&B.* The bigger the tree, the bigger the rootball. If different sizes of trees with the same or similar-sized rootballs are dug, the ones with larger tops may be less vigorous because of a poor root-to-top ratio. Before purchasing a balled-and-burlapped tree, untie the top of the burlap and examine the rootball carefully. Select one with a firm, solid ball of soil. Avoid trees with cracked or broken soil or circling roots at the soil surface.

Container-Grown Trees

Trees grown in containers offer the greatest uniformity and ease of handling. Nurseries find them easier to grow, in general, but must exercise skill and careful planning to ensure their vigor. Of a group of container-grown trees, a medium-sized tree stands the best chance of satisfactory performance. When buying, avoid trees with girdling (or circling) roots, as these indicate the tree has become too large for the container. Girdling roots are a common problem as more and more nursery trees are grown in containers, rather than transplanted from the ground. Select container-grown trees with strong, well-developed roots: Lift the tree slowly by grasping it at the base of the trunk. If the tree moves up before the can and soil do, this indicates a weak and underdeveloped root system. Avoid such specimens.

Roots

The quality of a tree's roots at the time of planting cannot be overstressed. Root defects can doom a tree to death or poor growth. The top of a young tree is not necessarily a good indicator of the quality of its root system.

A well-formed root system is symmetrically branched, with the main root growing down and out to provide trunk support. Container-grown and balled-and-burlapped trees should have fibrous roots that are developed enough that the rootball retains its shape and holds together when removed from the container or when the ball is moved. The main roots should be free of kinks (sharp bends in the roots) and circles (roots that wrap around themselves or the outside of the container).

Check for kinked or circling roots A healthy trunk flares at the soil line. The absence of a flare may indicate a girdling root. Brush away the soil from the top of the rootball, or stick your finger in the top 2 to 3 inches near the trunk. You can usually see or feel kinked or circling roots at the top of the rootball.

Kinked and circling roots, if not corrected, can cause such weakness that the tree will not be able to stand upright without support. Circling roots may girdle the trunk of the tree, restricting the movement of water, nutrients, and food, causing it to grow poorly and possibly to die.

Trunk

In general, select a tree with a straight, tapered trunk that can stand by itself. Note, however, that some types of trees naturally have multiple or crooked trunks. The trunk should bend evenly in the wind, like a fishing pole. Commonly the branches are all located along the top half of the trunk and the tree is tightly tied to a stake. An unstaked tree is a better choice than a staked one, but if you must buy a staked tree, select one that can stand by itself when the stake is removed. Read the section on staking before you buy (see pages 22 to 24). In trees with lower branches removed, be sure to protect the bare lower trunk from sunburn after the tree is planted (see page 22).

Check the trunk Untie the tree from its stake, and bend the top to one side. It should bend evenly along the trunk and return to within 20 to 30 degrees of vertical. If it doesn't, look for a stronger tree. Also look for bark abrasions before buying. The bark should be free of injury from staking or improper handling. Avoid buying sunburned trees. Split, flattened, or dull-colored bark indicates sunburn. Sunburned trunks are extremely slow to heal and are subject to borer infestation (see page 37).

CARE AFTER BUYING

It is just as important to take proper care of the tree after you purchase it as it is to choose and plant it properly. Keep it moist and cool (especially if it is a bare-root tree) to prevent buds from growing before the tree is planted.

Bare-Root Trees

Plant bare-root trees within two days of purchase. If planting must be delayed, gently pack the roots in moist sawdust and store the tree in the shade. Keep the roots cool and moist. Take care that they are not exposed to frost.

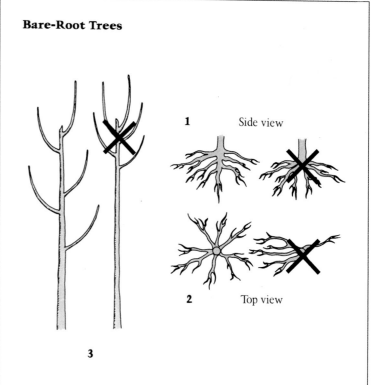

Bare-Root Trees

1

Side view

2

Top view

3

Select bare-root trees with several good-sized roots radiating outward at various levels from the main root (1) and in different directions (2). Try to find a tree whose leader has not been pruned. If the leader has been headed back, choose a tree with branches that alternate around the trunk and are well-spaced vertically (3).

Balled-and-Burlapped Trees

1   2   3

Before purchasing, untie the top of the burlap and look carefully at the rootball. Avoid specimens with cracked or broken soil (1). Select a tree with a firm, solid ball of soil (2). Look for circling roots at the soil surface (3). Select trees whose roots are free of kinks and circles (2).

Container-Grown Trees

1

2

3

Select container-grown trees with well-developed roots. Avoid specimens with circling or girdling roots (1). Lift the tree slowly, grasping it at the base (2). If the tree moves up before the container and soil do, the root system is inadequate. Trees should not bend when untied from the stake (3). Choose ones that can stand upright and that have lower lateral branches.

Bare-root trees can also be heeled in near the planting site for a short period. To heel in a bare-root tree, cover the roots with moist sawdust or soil, working it in around the roots to avoid air pockets. Heeling in is best done in a shaded area to prevent moisture loss and to keep buds dormant. If you must heel in the tree in the open, set it in a trench so that its top leans toward the southwest.

Balled-and-Burlapped Trees

Balled-and-burlapped trees can be bought and planted at any time of the year, although spring is best. Until planting, place the tree in the shade in an upright position. Keep the entire rootball slightly moist; water it slowly from the top. Also wet the foliage occasionally.

Container-Grown Trees

Trees in containers can be planted at any time of the year where the ground does not freeze. If you will not be planting the tree right away, keep the soil moist and wet the foliage occasionally. Shade the container by placing it behind a slanted board or by covering it with soil or sawdust. It is important to protect container-grown trees from the sun, as most containers are made of dark-colored materials. If plants in these dark containers are left exposed to the sun, soil temperatures near the side of the container can get high enough to injure or kill the roots.

PREPARING FOR PLANTING

A planting hole acts as a transition zone in which the roots of a tree adjust from the planting mix of the nursery to the soil of the garden. Most soils will provide a suitable rooting medium—one that holds moisture while allowing proper aeration—with little or no amending. You can improve soils that are extremely sandy or claylike by adding organic matter—compost, nutrified bark, or well-decomposed sawdust—at a rate of 2 parts soil to 1 part organic matter. If amendments to the soil are necessary, dig a larger planting hole to create a wider area of amended soil around the rootball. Otherwise, growing roots may remain in the amended soil, not penetrating into the surrounding unamended soil.

When planting trees from containers with a light, organic, soilless mix, amendments will help ease the transition to the surrounding, heavier garden soil.

When planting container-grown trees or balled-and-burlapped trees, make sure that the bottom of the hole is firm and level. A slight rise in the center makes it easier to spread the roots of bare-root trees.

Soil Compaction

The soil around new homes, former paths or drives, or old farmland may be severely compacted. In this case, make the planting hole large enough in diameter and deep enough to reach the soil below the compacted layer. For backfill, use surface soil or soil from below the compacted layer, mixed with a little organic matter. Rototill a wide area around the rootball to allow for eventual root growth.

Shallow Soils

Shallow soils may restrict growth and prevent the tree from anchoring fully. Such soil may be underlaid with rock or hardpan—a layer of fine clay particles that have accumulated some distance below the soil surface to form sedimentary rock. In shallow soils, water may collect on the impervious layer, where it may drown the roots of shrubs and trees.

To deepen shallow soil, break through the hardpan layer with a pick, posthole digger, or well auger. Use only surface soil (or surface soil mixed with organic matter) for backfill. Allow it to settle, and plant to the side of the drainage hole to prevent the tree from settling (see illustration).

When you can't go through the impervious layer, be sure there is sufficient soil depth to anchor a tree, and use a perforated drainage pipe to a gravel-filled sump or to a lower grade to remove excess water.

PLANTING

Several steps are involved in planting a tree properly. Problem roots must be pruned and removed. The rootball must be placed carefully in the hole. After planting, watering is essential for a healthy tree.

Although orientation is not necessarily critical to the survival of a tree, consider it before setting the tree in its hole. Point the lowest branches toward areas of little or no activity. If wind is a problem, place the side of the tree with the most branches into the wind.

Prepare the planting hole, place the rootball, add the backfill, and make a basin. Proper planting techniques will ensure a healthy and vigorous tree.

Drainage in Layered Soils

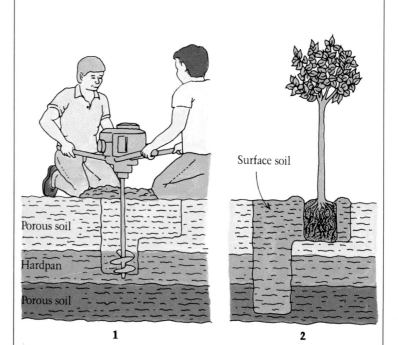

Porous soil

Hardpan

Porous soil

Surface soil

1   **2**

In soil underlaid with hardpan, drill a drainage hole offset from the planting hole to prevent settling. Drill through the impervious layer with a power posthole digger (1). Fill the drainage hole with surface soil, and plant in the planting hole as usual (2).

Preparing the Roots

Before planting, cleanly cut back any injured, diseased, twisted, or dead roots to healthy tissue. For container-grown trees, cut away some of any roots that are matted at the bottom or circling around the outside of the rootball. In freeing the roots at the edge of the rootball, also break away some of the soil to provide better contact between the roots and the fill soil. Comb all roots out away from the ball before planting.

Pruning the Top

Even if no roots are lost during planting, the top of the tree may still have such a large leaf area that frequent watering is needed to prevent wilting. Reduce the leaf area by thinning out branches that are close together, cross one another, or are broken. Prune both to remove leaf area and to establish tree structure and appearance. Avoid heading back (cutting back to a stub or a small lateral branch) or over-pruning the tree.

Bare-root trees will probably need more pruning than container-grown or balled-and-burlapped trees because they are dug up with fewer roots.

Some pruning may have been done at the nursery. If so, little more is necessary. Check for pruning scars, or ask the nursery.

Placing the Rootball

With balled-and-burlapped trees, fold back the burlap at least 2 inches below the soil level. Do not leave the burlap exposed, as it may draw moisture from the soil, drying it out faster than normal. Carefully slice the burlap on the sides and bottom of the rootball to allow for easy root penetration.

Burlap generally rots away within a year; however, some burlap is treated with a preservative for nursery keeping. Treated burlap, plastic, or other nonbiodegradable wraps must be removed before planting. Ask at the nursery whether the burlap has been treated. If it has, gently rock the rootball to one side, pushing the

Planting Bare-Root Trees

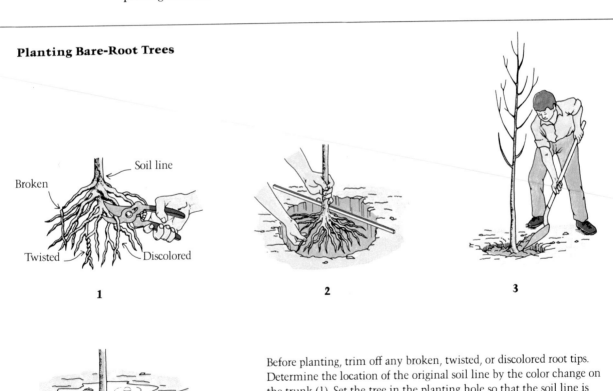

Broken

Soil line

Twisted

Discolored

1

2

3

4

Before planting, trim off any broken, twisted, or discolored root tips. Determine the location of the original soil line by the color change on the trunk (1). Set the tree in the planting hole so that the soil line is above the surrounding soil. Spread roots evenly (2). Work backfill soil around roots. Firm the soil gently as you fill the hole, making sure that roots and soil are in contact (3). Eliminate air pockets, settle soil, and bring soil into firm contact with the roots by running water slowly over the root area (4).

burlap as far under it as possible. Then rock it back, and the burlap should come free. With smaller rootballs, it may be easier just to lift the plant away from the burlap carefully.

Place the rootball on a firm base in the prepared hole. The soil line of the tree should be slightly higher than the surrounding soil. Remove any ties around the rootball. Spread the roots to provide good anchorage and to prevent circling.

Unless that soil is undesirable, backfill the hole with the original soil. For heavy, extremely light, or compacted soil, add organic matter. See page 18 for instructions on mixing backfill.

Don't put fertilizer in the planting hole or mix it with the backfill soil. This can injure the plant. Fertilize trees when new growth begins.

Work the soil in around the roots so that they are spreading and supported by soil underneath. After filling in 3 to 4 inches of soil, water the roots and allow the soil to settle in by gently rocking the tree back and forth.

The original soil level of the plant should be 1 to 2 inches above the soil level of the newly planted tree. If the trunk shows a dark-to-light color change at its base, this indicates the original soil level in the nursery.

Making a Basin

Make the watering basin for trees at least 30 inches in diameter or twice the size of the rootball, whichever is larger. A soil ridge 4 or 5 inches high around the perimeter makes it possible to wet the soil thoroughly.

Fill the basin with water to further settle the soil and to provide the roots with water. This will improve the contact between the fill soil and the roots.

After watering to settle the soil, check to be certain the original soil line on the tree is not buried. If a bare-root tree settles too low, grasp its trunk near the soil and carefully lift the tree an inch or two higher than the proper level, then let it settle back. This gives its roots better contact with the soil. With container or balled-and-burlapped trees, use a shovel under the rootball to raise it while lifting on the trunk. Raise it an inch or two above the proper level and let it settle back. Lift trees carefully: The higher the tree is raised, the closer the roots are drawn together. This weakens anchorage and may reduce contact between roots and soil.

Planting Balled-and-Burlapped Trees

Carefully set the wrapped rootball into the hole. The soil line of the tree should be slightly higher than the surrounding soil. Remove any ties around the rootball (1). Fill the hole with backfill soil, firming it down as you go (2). Cut the burlap away from the trunk, and be sure all edges are buried well below the soil surface (3).

Planting Container-Grown Trees

Gently knock the tree out of the container and remove circling or matted roots (1). Set the tree carefully into the hole. Be sure the soil line of the tree is slightly higher than the surrounding soil. Add and firm backfill soil gradually to assure good root contact (2).

For several weeks after planting, the rootball will need more frequent watering than the surrounding soil, which has few roots. In areas of lighter soil, make certain that the rootball receives adequate water by building a dike inside the first basin. It should be slightly smaller than the rootball itself. This inner circle will concentrate the water where it is needed. Water the inner circle thoroughly every one to three days for the first few weeks.

Later watering needs will depend on how many leaves the tree has, and on the weather. Check the moisture in the rootball by digging down a couple of inches to see if the soil is damp. After the roots penetrate the transition zone—four to six weeks after planting—remove the inner dike. In the meantime, the outer zone will need less water but must be kept moist. Where drainage is poor, avoid overwatering.

In areas of high rainfall, you may have to knock down the dikes temporarily to keep water from accumulating at the base of the tree. If dikes are left in place under these circumstances, crown rot can result, which may kill the tree.

Use tree wrap to prevent damage to newly planted trees from pests and yard-care equipment. Staking may also be necessary for proper support.

Wrapping the Trunk

Wrapping the trunk of a newly planted tree will help limit damage from insects, cats, children, rodents, and mowers. It will also prevent sunburn until the canopy develops enough shade and the bark enough toughness to withstand the heat of the sun.

Use burlap, paper grocery sacks, or special tree-wrap material available at garden stores. This material is made of two layers of crepe paper with a layer of asphalt in between and is cut into strips about 2 inches wide. Special tree-wrap material has the proper stretch and thickness.

Attach the wrap with masking tape, and work from just below ground level, where most borers enter, to the first of the major lateral branches. Wrap snugly in overlapping circles. Leave the wrap on until the tree leafs out in spring the first season after wrapping—leaving the wrap on too long can damage the tree.

Avoiding Competition From Turf

When trees are planted in a lawn area, keep the turf well away from the trunk of the tree during the first three years. The growth of young trees can be limited by grass growing close to their trunks, even if additional water and fertilizer are applied. Keeping a 30-inch-diameter area of bare soil around the tree will also help keep young trees from being damaged by lawn mowers. Damage to the trunks of young trees can dwarf or even kill them.

STAKING

A young tree that is exposed to wind and weather concentrates its energy on growing strong enough to remain upright. It develops a sturdy trunk that is tapered to bend without breaking, and a strong root system to hold this trunk in place. Unfortunately, some common practices prevent the young tree from growing as strong as it should. Nurseries try for a maximum use of space by placing trees too close together. Thus, the side branches, which could nourish the trunk and strengthen the tree, are shaded out or trimmed off. Then the tree is staked. These practices encourage height growth at the expense of trunk development. Often these trees cannot remain upright without a stake. Ideally, select an unstaked, sturdy tree with some side branches that will strengthen the trunk. If none is available, you can purchase a staked tree and restake it in the garden, but only until it is sufficiently established to stand on its own.

Sometimes thinning the top will be sufficient to reduce the weight and wind resistance. Try that before staking; it may result in a stronger tree.

Support stakes should be just high enough to hold the tree upright under calm conditions; the tree should return to a vertical position after bending in the wind.

Staking may also help to prevent damage from lawn mowers and other equipment; even a sturdy young tree may need protective stakes. In this case, place three stakes, several feet tall, at the outer edge of the rootball and at least 6 inches from the trunk.

Anchor Staking

The trunks of many trees will hold their tops upright as long as the roots are firmly anchored. Anchor stakes can be used to hold the roots where they are planted until they become established enough to hold the tree. Two or three short stakes will probably be sufficient to anchor the roots. Tie them to the trunk with loops of webbing or plastic tape. Remove ties after the first growing season, when roots have grown securely into the surrounding soil. Anchor stakes can be used both to protect the trunk and to hold the roots.

Staking to Support the Trunk

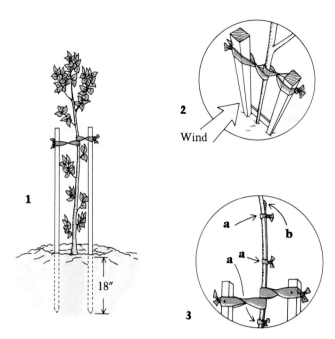

Tie the trunk to the stake(s) at only one level and within 2″ of the stake top. The tie should provide some flexibility but not enough that the tree rubs against the stake(s). Use rustproof tacks or staples to hold the ties in place on the stake. At least 18″ of the stake(s) should be below ground level to ensure stability (1). Stake the tree at a right angle to the strongest wind (2). An exceptionally spindly trunk may benefit from an auxiliary stake of spring-steel wire (3). Use polyethylene tape to hold the trunk to the wire (a), and wrap the top of the wire with tape as well (b). Remove the auxiliary stake as soon as possible—usually by the end of the first growing season.

Anchor Staking

Use two or three short stakes to anchor roots. Use loops of webbing or plastic tape to tie the stakes to the trunk. Remove the ties as soon as possible, no later than the end of the first growing season.

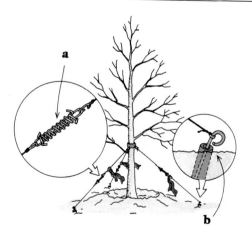

To anchor newly transplanted larger trees, attach guy wires to a soft collar around the trunk or to screw eyes. Use a compression spring on each wire for greater flexibility (a). Guy wires with pins that insert into buried pipes can be removed for lawn mowing (b). Tie rags to the wires for visibility.

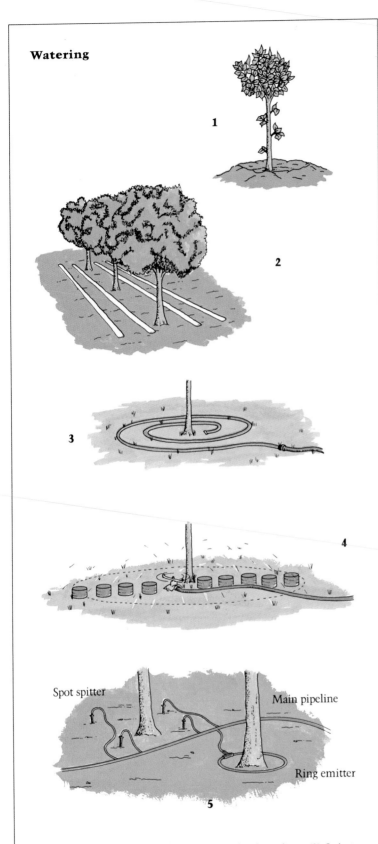

Watering

Use a shallow basin to water a young, newly planted tree (1). Irrigate rows of trees with parallel furrows on both sides (2). Distribute water evenly using a soaker hose around a tree (3). When using a sprinkler, measure the evenness and depth of its coverage with an array of cans (4). Use a drip system to keep trees moist with little wasted water (5).

Making Your Own Stakes

Either wood (2-by-2 boards) or metal (T-iron) can be used for protective, anchor, or support stakes. Metal stakes need a flange or plate just below the ground for extra stability.

Ties can be almost any soft, flexible material. Green or black ¼-inch polyethylene tape is commonly used. Don't use thin materials such as fishing line, twine, or, worst of all, wire. Any friction will cause these materials to cut deep into the bark, seriously damaging the tree. Loop guy wires, used to anchor larger trees, through a soft collar, such as old garden hose, to protect the trunk of the tree (see illustration, page 23).

Removing Stakes

Use support and anchor staking as a temporary measure, and remove these stakes as soon as the tree is able to stand safely on its own. Stakes are usually needed only through the first season. Check deciduous trees to see if they can stand alone at the beginning of the dormant season (the end of autumn), but don't remove the ties until growth has begun in the spring. Leave the ties on in the interim to prevent the tree from being broken by winter storms.

WATERING

Trees, like all plants, require water for growth. They get water from the soil and lose most of it through their leaves by transpiration. Water is supplied by either rain or irrigation. How much water is available to a particular tree depends on the depth and spread of its roots. In most soils, most of a tree's feeder roots are located within 12 inches of the surface. When there is sufficient water, much of the water a tree uses is supplied from the top foot of soil. In times of drought, deep-rooted plants draw some water from lower roots.

During dry periods, or in areas where irrigation is necessary, watch trees closely to determine when they need water. Signs of water stress include wilting, a change in leaf color (from shiny to dull, or from dark green to gray-green), and premature leaf fall.

There are a number of ways to water efficiently: basins, furrows (for rows of trees), sprinklers, soakers, or drip systems (see illustration). The most important goals are to eliminate runoff, to confine water inside the drip line of branches, and to apply water uniformly.

FERTILIZING

Before applying any fertilizer, perform or commission a soil test to determine soil type and needs. Fertilizing with nitrogen can make young trees grow more rapidly and reach landscape size more quickly. In most soils mature trees need little or no fertilization as long as they have good leaf color and grow reasonably well. In fact, increased vigor may needlessly increase the size of trees and the density of the leaves. Leaves on the inside of such trees, or the plants under them, grow poorly because of heavy shade.

Apply nitrogen carefully, following package directions. Choose a fertilizer that is 50 percent nitrogen in slow-release form. Because nitrogen is transient, apply the necessary amount at two intervals; one half in spring and the other half in the autumn is often recommended.

Keep the fertilizer at least 6 inches away from the trunk to avoid injuring the tree. After application, sprinkle the area with water to wash the fertilizer into the soil. This begins the conversion of the less soluble forms of nitrogen and avoids burning the grass if the tree is planted near a lawn.

How much fertilizer should you apply? Let the trees be your guide. If growth is excessive on young trees, cut back the amount of fertilizer used or stop fertilizing altogether. If shoot growth is shorter than you want and leaf color is pale, carefully increase the rate. As trees mature, fertilizer is seldom, if ever, needed.

MULCHING

A mulch is any material that is put on the soil to cover and protect it. Mulches can do many things. They reduce moisture loss, improve soil structure, reduce soil erosion, impede soil compaction, keep weeds down, moderate soil temperatures, and provide a clean, firm surface for walking on during rainy weather.

Most mulches are the by-product of industry, agriculture, or your own gardening. Many are plant based and include wood shavings, wood chips, twigs, bark, aged sawdust, pine needles, shredded leaves, grass, rice hulls, corncobs, cocoa hulls, and pomace.

Prepare the area for mulching by bringing the soil to uniform grade and removing weeds. Apply mulch 3 inches thick. Keep mulch 6 inches from trunks. Putting medium-sized gravel, coarse sand, or cinders between the

trunk and the mulch will keep both the mulch and hungry rodents away from the trunk.

Bacteria and fungi that break down organic mulch require nutrients such as nitrogen and can actually cause a nutritional deficiency for the tree. Fertilize more frequently when using plant-based mulches.

A single sheet of black plastic placed on the ground around a tree can eliminate the need for further weed control, but it will reduce oxygen penetration and slow a tree's growth. Cut holes in the plastic so that water and oxygen can penetrate to tree roots. Improve its appearance by covering it with an organic mulch or crushed rock. Landscape fabric will serve the same purpose and is porous, so it will not reduce a tree's oxygen or water supply.

PRUNING

Pruning can do much to enhance the health and appearance of a tree. At planting time, light pruning helps compensate for the root loss of bare-root plants and improves the water balance in container-grown trees. Pruning can be used to encourage strong branch structure and handsome form. Regular maintenance pruning, such as removing dead wood and crossed

Some trees can be pruned and trained to grow flat against a support. This is called an espalier.

branches, lets light into the interior of the tree and will improve overall growth and vigor. Pruning is particularly useful for controlling tree size. On mature trees, pruning can be used to maintain a balance between vegetative growth and flowering. Stagnated trees can sometimes be revived through pruning.

A knowledge of how trees develop and how they respond to pruning is essential to knowing when and how to prune.

Why Prune?

Removing leafy shoots and buds that would become leaves allows the roots (which are not immediately affected) to supply the remaining parts of the tree with more water and nutrients. Pruning stimulates shoots to grow more rapidly and later into the season and causes leaves to become larger and darker green.

Although leaves will be larger and shoots longer, the total amount of leaf area and new growth will be less on a pruned tree. Because fewer leaves will be working, the result will be less total growth and less food stored.

The amount of both invigoration and dwarfing depends on the severity of the pruning. Removing dead, weak, and heavily shaded branches has little influence on growth,

Top: Through careful pruning and maintenance, some trees can be miniaturized. Shown here is a bonsai atlas cedar. Bottom: Topiary is the art of training, cutting, and pruning trees into ornamental shapes.

whereas the pruning of healthy branches that are well exposed to light can have a significant effect.

Thinning

The best method of tree pruning, thinning (or thinning out) involves removing a particular branch at its origin or cutting back to another lateral branch. Thinning can be used to accentuate a tree's beauty and form. The new growth follows the tree's natural branching pattern and tends to be more evenly distributed. Thinning creates a less dense and more open canopy. Because more light penetrates through the leaves, interior foliage and plants under the tree will grow better. A thinned tree is also less vulnerable to wind and storm damage.

Top: Pollarding, cutting a tree back to the trunk to promote a dense head of foliage, is seen in some formal gardens. Here, sycamore trees have been pollarded. Bottom: Branches like those of the American hornbeam, shown here, can be pleached, or woven, to create a shady arbor.

Pruning Conifers

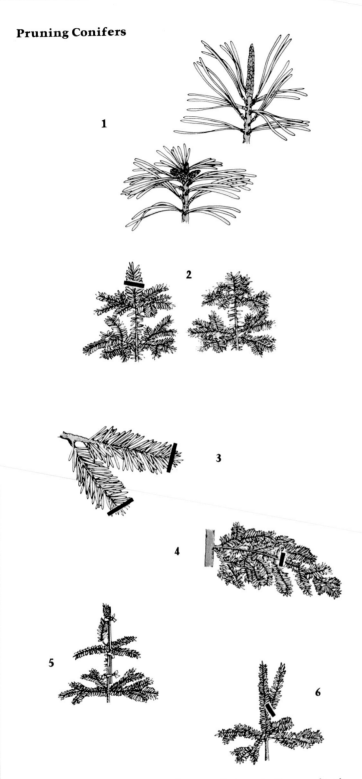

To make pines more compact and to control size, cut off some of each candle in late spring (1). Reduce open spaces in spruce by trimming off half of each of the terminal shoots in the spring when new needles are forming (2). Pinch terminal buds to keep conifer branches short (3). Shorten long branches to an inner lateral (4). Train a top lateral to replace a lost leader when necessary (5). When two leaders are competing, remove the less desirable one (6).

Pruning Conifers

Conifers do not need to be pruned as much as broadleaf trees. Prune them primarily to remove dead wood, to control size and shape (see illustration), or to reduce wind resistance. Most conifers do not have latent buds on wood without foliage; if this wood is cut back to a stub, no new growth follows. Exceptions are yew, arborvitae, sequoia, some junipers, and some pines.

Conifers typically have a central leader with branches radiating either at random or in vertical whorls around the trunk. Random-branching conifers—arborvitae, sequoia, and yew, for example—can be sheared or tip-pinched to control size and shape. Whorl-branching species—fir, pine, and spruce, for example—will form closer whorls if new growth is headed back to a bud.

To train columnar conifers, cut upright branches back to short, spreading laterals, or, in large specimens, head widely spreading branches just inside the desired foliage line of the column. Lost leaders on conifers can be replaced (see illustration).

The Pruning Process

To be most effective, prune broadleaf trees in the following order.
• First, prune away any dead, diseased, or crisscrossing branches.
• Next, prune for form. Make the smallest cuts first, and the largest ones last.

Small stems and shoots Using pruning shears, cut just above a healthy lateral bud to remove unwanted growth. Cut ¼ inch above the bud from which you want a branch to grow—more will leave a dead stub, less may damage the bud. Place the shears so that the blade cuts upward. Slant the cut upward toward the top of the bud, with the angle in the direction you want the new branch to grow.

Small branches Prune branches up to 1¼ inches thick with lopping shears. Again, cut upward; this both makes cutting easier and reduces the danger of bark tearing as the limb falls. Cut small limbs, including suckers (vigorous sprouts that grow from below a graft union or from the ground) and water sprouts (similar to suckers, but higher on the trunk), as close to the trunk or branch as possible.

Pruning Larger Branches With a Saw

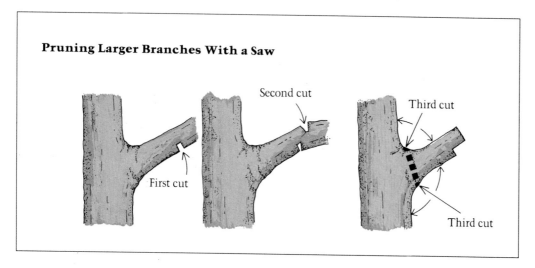

Second cut

First cut

Third cut

Third cut

Larger branches A handsaw will work on any branch thicker than 1¼ inches. If a branch is too heavy to support with your free hand, first make a rough cut about 6 inches from the trunk, and then cut off the 6-inch stub next to the trunk. This method keeps the bark from being stripped off the tree should the heavy branch slip from your hand while you're still cutting. To reach high branches, use a three-legged pruning ladder—tied to a nearby branch for extra stability. For branches more than 3 to 4 inches thick, use a wide-blade, single-edged saw and make three cuts as follows (also see illustration).

1. Make the first cut about one third of the way through the underside of the limb, about 3 feet from where it attaches to the trunk.

2. Make a second cut at the upper side of the branch, about 6 inches nearer the end of the branch than the first cut. The limb will then fall away without tearing the bark.

3. Make a third cut where the limb attaches to the trunk, at the collar of the branch, to remove the remaining stub. The collar is usually indicated by circular marks around the base of the branch. If you can't find these rings, cut from the top angle of attachment to the bottom angle of attachment.

Until recent research proved the method to be damaging, the common practice was to cut branches as flush as possible to the trunk, without leaving a trace of a stub. Now, however, experts recommend that the branch be cut just outside the branch collar. The resulting wound will be smaller and not quite as flush, but will be at the point where the tree can best seal off or compartmentalize the damaged wood and resume healthy growth.

Proper Pruning Cut   Improper Cuts

¼"

1   2   3   4

Cut back to a side bud where possible. A proper cut is at an angle about ¼" above the bud (1). Improper cuts are too far from the bud (2), at too sharp an angle (3), and too close to the bud (4).

Cutting Too Close   Cutting Too Far

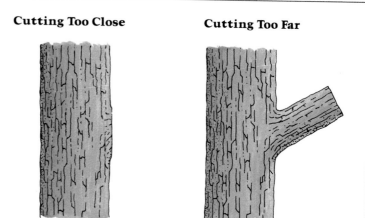

Cut branches just outside the branch collar for best sealing and to ensure resumption of healthy growth.

Branch Strength

Certain branch characteristics contribute to the structural strength of the trunk and the tree's major limbs. Branches that are attached to the tree at 45- to 90-degree angles are stronger than those attached at narrower angles. A wide angle allows strong connective wood to form in the crotches, on the sides, and on the lower portion of the branch. In training a young tree, select wide-angled branches to be the main scaffold branches, and remove those with narrow crotches while they are still small.

Relative branch size　For proper support, branches should be smaller than the trunk or limb they are growing on. Wherever two branches fork, the supporting branch should be larger than the other. Relative branch size is an important factor in the strength of branch attachments.

If the branch is too large in relation to the trunk or its supporting branch, slow the growth of the secondary branch until the trunk or supporting branch is larger. To do so, remove some of the twigs on the oversized branch by cutting back to a lateral.

Branch Spacing

The spacing of vertical branches can determine both structural strength and the shape of the tree. Unpruned trees of many species often have the more vigorous branches naturally well spaced and need little or no pruning. Where pruning is required, prune to ensure sufficient distance between scaffolds.

In addition to even vertical spacing, branches should be distributed evenly around the trunk; for example, there should be five to seven scaffold branches spaced in one or two rotations around the trunk, like an ascending spiral. A perfect spiral is not necessary for the tree to be well shaped and for the branches to be healthy and strong. The purpose is to prevent one branch from growing directly over another to the detriment of both—the upper one suffers from the extra competition for water and nutrients, and the lower one gets shaded out. Remove the less desirable branch of the two. Also, it is usually best not to have two branches opposite each other.

Training a Young Tree

Two things determine how a tree should be pruned—its landscape use and the natural growth habit of the tree. Mature trees can be pruned to suit a particular landscape use, but it is preferable to start with a young tree. Before pruning, decide how you want a tree to function in the landscape. Will it frame an attractive view or screen out an unattractive one? Do

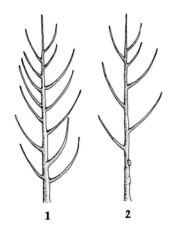

Thinning a Young Tree

When thinning a young tree, leave more scaffold branches than eventually will be needed (1). Select the most desirable permanent branches as the tree grows (2).

Inducing Lateral Branches

A nonbranching leader can be pinched during the growing season to induce the development of laterals. Two pinches, over two seasons, can produce branches at the height desired. (Leaves have been left off the illustration for clarity.)

you want low branches so that children can climb the tree or a high canopy to shade the house and patio?

Prune trees only enough to direct their growth effectively and to correct any structural weaknesses. Select sturdy branches with wide angles of attachment to be permanent scaffolds.

During each growing season, leave more shoots than you ultimately will select as permanent branches. After the second growing season, you will be able to choose from more developed branches.

Pruning During the Growing Season

During the growing season, pruning can often be done with just a little careful pinching. Pinch the leader to force more laterals, or pinch back laterals that threaten to dominate the leader. Pinch back, or cut off altogether, shoots that are too low, too close together, or in competition with branches you want to encourage. Pinching as little as 1 inch is enough to check growth temporarily so that selected limbs will develop properly. There will be little or no setback to the tree if this pinching is done before the shoots are 5 inches long. It also reduces the necessity of removing large branches later. Growth will be channeled where you want it.

If the tree is a species that does not branch on current growth, induce branching by pinching the leader at the height at which you want the first branch. On a vigorous tree, pinching new shoots will give you several well-spaced branches in one season, instead of a tall, unbranched whip.

Temporary Branches

Small, temporary branches along the trunk help strengthen the tree and shade it from sunburn. Shoots along the trunk will increase its diameter and taper, resulting in a stronger tree overall.

Temporary branches should be about 4 to 12 inches apart and should be kept short by pinching. This is one place where you want weak growth. Choose the less vigorous shoots along the trunk for temporary branches.

As the young tree develops a sturdy trunk and permanent lower branches, the temporary branches can be reduced and eventually

Pruning Spring-Flowering Trees

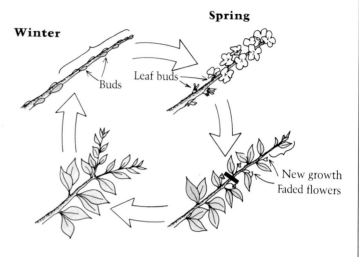

Prune trees that flower in the spring from buds on one-year-old wood, especially flowering fruit trees, at or near the end of the bloom period. Do not prune in fall or winter, as this will remove buds that would flower in the spring.

Pruning Summer-Flowering Trees

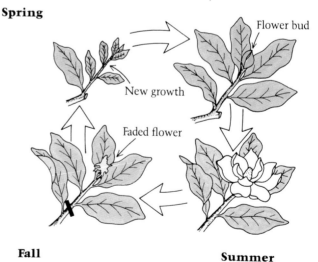

Prune summer-flowering trees in late fall to early spring, before growth starts. Pruning new growth removes shoots on which flowers may develop.

eliminated. You can begin reducing their number after two or three years, when the trunk is 2 to 3 inches in diameter for small trees, 5 to 6 inches for trees that will get larger. Remove them over a period of two to three years, each time pruning out the largest ones.

Maintaining a Leader

Sometimes a leader loses its control and is overtaken by one or more upright laterals. If the leader cannot be saved without severe pruning, choose the lateral in the best position and thin the leader back to it. Other laterals may need to be pruned to ensure that the new leader will dominate.

If the leader is damaged and must be removed and you want the tree to develop a natural, pyramidal, central leader shape, select a side branch near the top and tie it to other branches or to a stick or stake positioned alongside the tree trunk to hold the new leader in place. If necessary, cut other laterals back enough to make the desired leader dominant (see illustration).

Pruning Mature Trees

A tree's scaffold limbs and its main structure have usually been selected by the third or fourth year, depending on the kind of tree and its growing conditions. If the scaffolds are well placed, the tree may need little or no pruning for several years.

There are several reasons why mature trees may need to be pruned. Tree health and appearance can be improved by the removal of limbs that are dead, weak, diseased, or insect infested. Remove broken, low, and crossing limbs for appearance and safety.

You can emphasize the structural features of a tree by moderate thinning to open the tree to view. To open up a medium- to large-sized tree (40 to 60 feet), cut moderate-sized limbs (1 to 2 inches in diameter). For smaller trees, cut smaller limbs around the tops and sides of the tree. Remove branches that are close to others. Cutting branches in larger trees should be necessary only if the tree has not been properly pruned in the past or if its use in the landscape is changing.

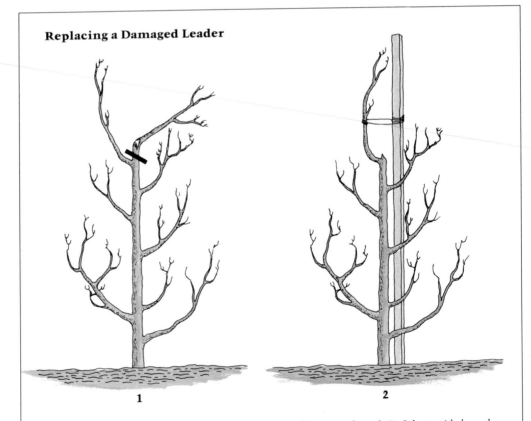

Replacing a Damaged Leader

1

2

Remove a broken or damaged leader and replace it with a strong lateral (1). Select a side branch near the top of the tree and tie it to other branches or to a stake positioned along the tree trunk (2). Cut back competing laterals.

REPAIRING BROKEN LIMBS

When a limb is broken, cut it back to solid wood as soon as possible, following proper pruning techniques (see pages 28 and 29). If the branch is small, use sharp pruning shears to make a slanting cut just above a healthy bud on the outside of the branch (see illustration, page 29). The branch that grows from this outside bud will naturally grow away from the trunk, forming an open, graceful shape, instead of inward toward the tree center, causing crowding.

If a larger limb is broken, use a saw to cut back to the nearest branch collar. Make three cuts on these larger limbs, following proper pruning procedures (see page 29), so that the weight of the limb will not tear away healthy bark that should be left intact.

A cut or wounded tree, unique in this respect among plants, will develop callus tissue that will eventually close the wound. Through a process called compartmentalization (see page 29), a tree also forms a barrier zone, isolating the wound from healthy tissue.

If a branch is broken but the bark is intact for at least a third of the way around the branch, it may be possible to save the branch. Splint the branch into position with two boards bound to support the break (see illustration). If branch strength is important, however, remove the limb; it will never be as strong as before the break.

HANDLING TRUNK DAMAGE

Sometimes larger limbs that have not been shaped or braced will break, tearing away part of the trunk (see illustration). These branches must be removed completely with as clean a cut as possible. A trunk wound is less threatening if less of the circumference of the tree is involved. Use a mallet and sharp chisel to trim away all loose bark, and round off the upper and lower ends of the wound. This shape makes it easier for water to run out, for the sap flow to pass more easily around the interruption, and for callus tissue to grow over the wound.

Small splits that occur as the tree develops—sometimes called growth splits—are generally shallow and tend to callus quickly, needing no special treatment.

Frost cracks, another common trunk injury, will usually callus over during the next growing season. Do not fill them.

Repairing a Broken Limb

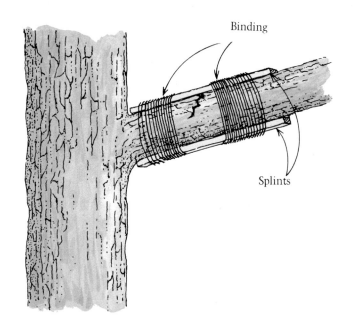

Some broken branches can be saved by splinting. Splints should be long (3 to 5 times the diameter of the branch) for adequate leverage and support.

Shaping a Trunk Wound

 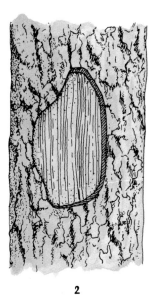

If a part of the trunk is torn or wounded (1), proper shaping will speed callusing. Carefully remove only the damaged bark. Do not greatly enlarge the wound. Keep the scribing shallow and round off the points (2).

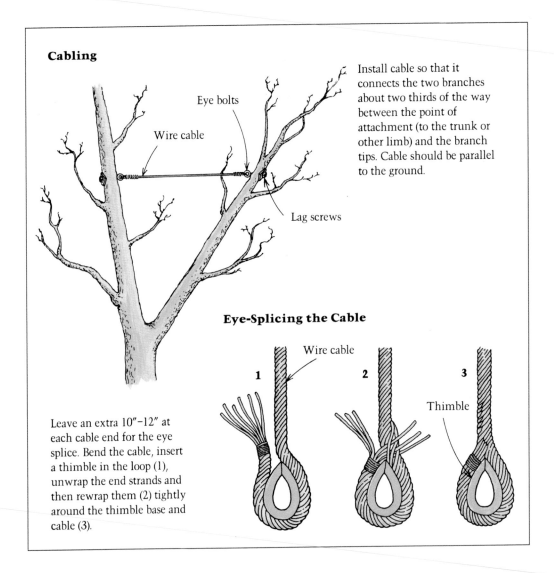

Cabling

Eye bolts

Wire cable

Lag screws

Install cable so that it connects the two branches about two thirds of the way between the point of attachment (to the trunk or other limb) and the branch tips. Cable should be parallel to the ground.

Eye-Splicing the Cable

Wire cable

1   2   3

Thimble

Leave an extra 10″–12″ at each cable end for the eye splice. Bend the cable, insert a thimble in the loop (1), unwrap the end strands and then rewrap them (2) tightly around the thimble base and cable (3).

CABLING

Cabling is used as a safety measure if a branch with a weak angle of attachment threatens to split from a tree (see illustration). Although cabling and bracing should be performed by a professional, knowing the proper method will help you judge whether the work is done correctly.

For best results, the cables should connect the two branches about two thirds of the way between the point of attachment and the branch tips. Use lag screws, eyebolts, thimbles, and wire cable (select the diameter depending on the weight it must support). Put the cables where they will not cause rubbing or abrasions to any limbs. Place the anchor points on each branch at the same distance from the angle of attachment so that the cable will be parallel to the ground.

Drill holes in the limbs and insert the lag screws or bolts. Draw the limbs together with rope to hold them in place and to prevent slack in the cable once installed. Measure the cable, leaving an extra 10 to 12 inches at each end for the eye splice. Bend the cable at the point of attachment, insert a thimble into the loop, unwrap the strands of the end, and wrap them tightly around the thimble base and cable to make a secure attachment. Do the same at the other end.

Next, attach the cable to the lag screw or eyebolt. When the cable is in place, remove the rope. A leaning tree can be cabled to another tree for support in the same way.

HANDLING ROOT PROBLEMS

Anything that circles a tree can stunt or kill it, including its own roots. As roots increase in size as the tree is growing, the stunting caused by circling roots is compounded. Proper planting is the best means of preventing such problems.

In any case, if a tree is failing to thrive, check for a girdling root at the surface or slightly below. Cut girdling roots carefully, using a saw, an ax, or a mallet and chisel, as close as possible to the point where they connect with the tree (see illustration, page 36). Removing these cut roots can be difficult and is not necessary, as they will wither over time.

Because most of a tree's roots are often within 12 inches of the soil surface, any digging, soil compaction, building, or cementing of areas near a tree may result in root damage. To avoid harming roots when laying trenches for utility or other lines, use (or request the use of) tunneling equipment that will work beneath large roots. If there is no way to avoid some root damage, consult a tree care professional for ways to help the tree compensate before it shows signs of distress.

Preventing Animal Damage

Wrapping the trunk of a young tree will do much to ward off damage from gnawing mice, scratching cats, and leg-lifting dogs. Keep mulch material pulled back about 6 inches from the base of the trunk to discourage burrowing mice.

Where rabbits are a problem, add a loose cylinder of hardware cloth (small-mesh plastic or wire screen) before winter starts and bark becomes the prime source of food. If the snow get very deep, pull these cylinders up above the snowline as needed.

Ecologically sound sprays are available that will penetrate the plant tissue with a taste and scent that repels animals. These should not be used on fruit trees or other edible plants, however, as they may affect the flavor. Read labels carefully for restrictions.

Wrapped bars of strong-scented soap loosely tied to young fruit trees may discourage deer from eating the bark, leaves, or fruit.

Large animals can damage or kill small trees in many ways. To get trees started in pastures, it is necessary to fence them in until they are large and sturdy.

Protecting Roots

When adding fill, do not add any over the root zone. If fill is necessary, make a well around the trunk. Layer soil, fabric, and coarse gravel to allow for aeration. Build a pipeline for proper air circulation and drainage.

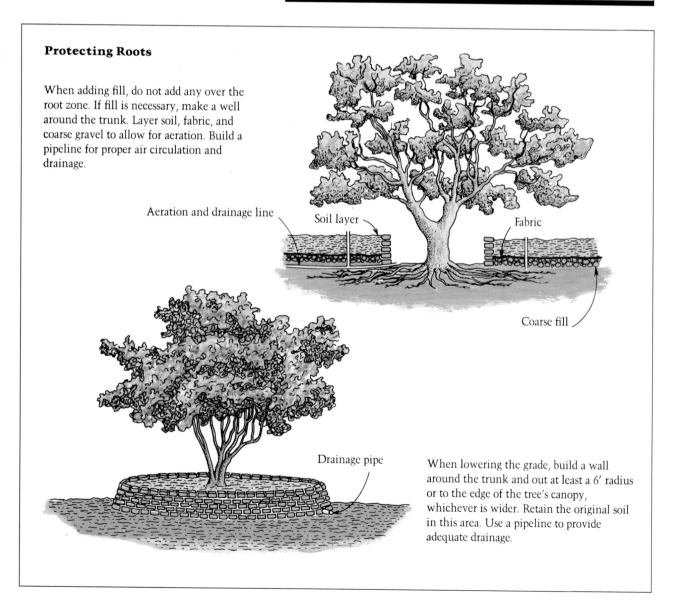

Aeration and drainage line

Soil layer

Fabric

Coarse fill

Drainage pipe

When lowering the grade, build a wall around the trunk and out at least a 6' radius or to the edge of the tree's canopy, whichever is wider. Retain the original soil in this area. Use a pipeline to provide adequate drainage.

Getting Professional Help

Homeowners can handle many tree problems themselves. They can make a major difference in the health and welfare of all their trees by observing and identifying problems early. But most people just do not have the knowledge, the equipment, or the agility to treat large trees, the very trees that add value, beauty, and comfort and whose cost of removal usually well exceeds the cost of treatment.

For larger trees or when tree problems are difficult to treat, seek help from a professional arborist. Your local nursery or garden center may be able to recommend a responsible arborist. If the International Society of Arboriculture has a certification program in your state, contact them for the name of a certified arborist. In states that have no licensing, even unqualified people can call themselves arborists.

Do not hesitate to ask about training, experience, or references. Consider visiting a local job site at which the arborist in question has worked. Be sure the arborist carries sufficient and current insurance and that this person's working methods are safe. An arborist's first concern should be saving your trees, although an experienced professional should know when it might be better to remove a declining tree and replace it with a new, young tree.

Cutting Girdling Roots

Girdling roots stunt a tree's growth. They will often constrict the trunk, preventing its natural flare. Cut them carefully as close as possible to the point where they connect with the tree.

REMOVING TREES AND STUMPS

Young trees that die can be pulled or cut off at soil level. Unless you are absolutely sure of the cause of death and it is not soil transmitted, it is best not to plant a similar tree in the same location.

Large trees should be removed if they are dead, in danger of falling, diseased to the point of contamination, or if they are crowding other, more choice trees. It takes special equipment and experience to remove large trees, and most homeowners should leave the job to a professional.

Discuss stump-removal options with a professional arborist also. You can remove smaller stumps by severing the roots and rocking the stump loose from the hole. For instant removal, some tree care companies have a stump grinder that will turn a stump into a pile of wood chips that can be used for mulch on the rest of the garden. You can also plant vines (such as Virginia creeper) to spread over and hide the stump. Vines screen and soften the sight, and the rootlets and moisture contribute to the natural process of decay.

MOVING LARGE TREES

If a tree with special appeal or great value is not where you want it to be, consider moving it. Moving a large, mature tree from one location to another is much costlier in the short term than growing a new one, but the years of enjoyment and growth are beyond price. Modern tree spades that encircle a tree with mechanical blades and then lift it with a cone of soil and roots make it possible to move fairly large trees with a high rate of success. If you can get your hands around the trunk of a tree, it can probably be moved if there is sufficient access area to get the spade in place. Nursery operators, landscape contractors, arborists, or other tree professionals may offer this service. It is best done in late fall to early spring when trees are dormant.

If you don't want to go to the expense of moving a tree but believe that the tree may have value to someone else, contact a local nursery, tree care service, or landscape contractor. They may be glad to move it for you to the yard of an appreciative customer who is quite willing to pay for the service.

TREE INSECTS AND DISEASE

Proper care will do much to reduce tree problems, but even trees that are well adapted and well maintained may be affected by pests or disease at some point in their lives. Early detection of such problems is the best hope for easy handling. Be aware of any visible change in a tree's leaves, bark, or structure. It is often wise to consult a professional before embarking on a treatment program, especially with older, larger trees. See page 36 for information on how to find a qualified arborist.

The following are some common tree pests and control methods. Although many problems and treatments are best handled by experts, knowing what to look for and how to treat it will help you manage your valuable trees. Spraying is not always recommended, but in cases where applications of this nature are called for, read and follow all label directions carefully. Many sprays are toxic to people, animals, beneficial insects, and plants.

Anthracnose

This term refers to several different fungi that can infect the leaves of maple, ash, sycamore, oak, and linden trees, among others. These fungi produce small brown spots that may coalesce. This gives a scorched appearance to the entire leaf, and affected leaves may drop off the tree. Usually young leaves and tender shoots are affected, particularly in a wet spring. A second crop of leaves and twigs will often fall prey to anthracnose as well. Groups of brushlike, weak stems often develop due to the repeated cycle of defoliation.

Control The best means of control is a thinned tree canopy that allows for better air circulation. Trees should also be well fertilized and growing vigorously. Anthracnose is generally not life threatening to the tree, and spray treatments with fungicides such as chlorothalonil, captan, or benomyl are recommended only in severe cases.

Beetles

There are many leaf-eating beetles. Two of the most destructive are the elm leaf beetle and the Japanese beetle. Elm leaf beetles skeletonize leaves. Infested elms can be completely defoliated—a situation that leads to further harm by inviting borers.

The Japanese beetle (usually not found in the West) is a ½-inch-long, metallic-green beetle with a coppery back. These beetles can damage whole groves of trees by eating leaves, leaving only the veined skeleton.

Control Spray with acephate (Orthene®), carbaryl (Sevin®), or diazinon when the damage is first noticed, and repeat as necessary. Follow label directions carefully. Beetle larvae (also called grubs) present in the lawn can be controlled with milky spore, a bacterial organism.

Borers

Any tree—especially birch and mountain ash—that is in a weakened or stressed condition will attract borers. Drought, sunburn, frost cracks, poor soil, bark injury, and air pollution are some of the major causes of stress and, consequently, of borer attack. Damage includes

Left: Anthracnose
Right: Beetles

structural weakening, death by girdling the cambium layer, and vulnerability to disease organisms. Holes in the bark indicating the presence of borers may be very tiny or up to 1 inch in diameter; they may be round or oval.

Control As a preventive measure, do everything possible to reduce tree stress. Wrapping the trunk of a tree can help prevent a borer

Top: Borers
Center: Cankers
Bottom: Caterpillars

infestation. Insecticides such as lindane and chlorpyrifos will control some types of borers. Before applying determine borer type to ensure effective control.

Cankers

These are dead and diseased areas that develop on trees, usually on woody branches or trunks. A common symptom is dieback starting at branch tips and sunken lesions on the branches and twigs. Virtually all plants can be attacked by canker-forming diseases.

Control Prune and discard infected branches. Paint pruning wounds with a disinfectant. When trunks are seriously invaded, often the tree cannot be saved.

Some cankers bleed (ooze). Maples, elms, birches, and low-vigor trees are particularly susceptible to canker bleeding. To best control this, restore the tree's health by supplying proper water and fertilizer. Control insects, and prune in late winter when bleeding is reduced. Cut cankerous areas back to healthy bark so that callus tissue can form.

Caterpillars

Moths and butterflies are harmless creatures, but their larvae—tent caterpillars, bagworms, and loopers (or cankerworms), to name just a few—are some of the most damaging leaf-eating pests.

Control Use *Bacillus thuringiensis* (Bt), an organic, bacteria-based compound, to control caterpillars. Use insecticides such as acephate (Orthene®), carbaryl (Sevin®), diazinon, or malathion only where infestations are severe. Follow label instructions carefully.

Honeydew

Some insects, such as aphids, that feed on trees by sucking their sap excrete honeydew, a sticky, clear, sugary material. Large numbers of ants, flies, and even honeybees, all of which are attracted to honeydew, are indicators of the presence of these pests. In time, a sooty mold may grow on the honeydew, blackening the leaves of infested plants. Soft scales and leafhoppers are also common honeydew excreters. Though unsightly, the honeydew seldom does permanent damage.

Control Use insecticidal soap to control these pests. These soaps can burn the tree, however, so follow label instructions carefully and test them first on an unimportant branch.

Fire Blight

This is a bacterial disease that affects many plants of the rose family, including crab apples, hawthorn, loquat, and mountain ash. Fire blight survives in cankers, leaves, and previously blighted fruits. Usually it is spread by splashing water, flies, and other insects during the bloom period, gaining entry through flowers and wounds. Symptoms are the sudden wilting of leaves, which then turn dark, as if burned. Leaves hang on rather than fall.

Control A weak bordeaux, copper, or strepto-mycin spray applied during bloom will prevent the disease. First spray when 10 percent of the flowers are open. Repeat every five to seven days during the blooming period. Prune out diseased wood, cutting several inches below the infected parts into healthy wood. Sterilizing pruning tools after each cut in a solution of household bleach (9 parts water to 1 part bleach) can prevent further spread of the disease during pruning.

Powdery Mildew

This fungus disease causes an unsightly, grayish, powdery coating to form on young shoots, leaves, and flower buds. It thrives in shade and where air circulation is poor. This disease attacks many shade and flowering trees.

Control In most cases powdery mildew does not cause long-term damage. However, spraying with chlorothalonil, lime-sulfur, triforine, or benomyl may prevent this disease. To apply follow label directions precisely.

Scale

These are small, sucking insects. They are immobile except when in the "crawler" stage, which occurs after the eggs hatch, usually in the spring. There are many types of scales that can damage trees. If left unchecked, scales can build up large populations that can weaken or even cause the death of trees.

Control A dormant oil spray applied in late winter or early spring smothers scales or their eggs with a thin layer of oil. Acephate (Orthene®), carbaryl (Sevin®), diazinon, or malathion can be used in summer when the crawlers appear.

Tree Selection Guide

Trees can be chosen based on the amount of space available for their growth, on their tolerance of adverse conditions (flooding, pests, sea winds), and for their visual appeal. Some trees offer nuts or fruit, others spring flowers, and still others beautiful fall color. This chapter includes lists of trees for specific uses, from summer-flowering trees to small-space trees to trees that attract birds.

I n choosing appropriate trees, gardeners are faced with a number of considerations, including water needs, soil requirements, speed of growth, and ultimate height. However, the most important aspect of selecting a tree is its tolerance for cold. All trees have a minimum temperature below which they cannot survive. Some trees also have a limit to the amount of heat they can withstand, and they should not be grown in areas where the temperatures consistently rise above this limit.

The United States Department of Agriculture (USDA) has developed a simple system in which the United States and southern Canada are divided into climate zones according to their lowest recorded winter temperatures. Listed with each tree included in this chapter are the zones it will grow in. These zones are a general guide only; climates often vary within zones. There are a number of reasons for this: Large bodies of water, snow cover, soil types, slope of the land, elevation, and air circulation will all influence climate. If you have a question about the hardiness of the tree you wish to plant, be sure to check with a local nursery or county extension agent.

Mixed evergreen and deciduous trees create an attractive and varied winter scene around this home.

Ilex opaca
(American holly)

GENERAL CLIMATE CONSIDERATIONS

South- and west-facing slopes are always warmer than north- and east-facing slopes because they absorb more of the sun's radiant energy. Thermal belts are warm microclimates that develop on sloping land above valleys and other lowlands. These bands of mild temperatures are localized; both above and below them, winters are distinctly colder. If your garden is in a warm thermal belt, you probably will be able to grow some trees considered too cold intolerant for the general area.

Structural walls, hedges, and screens can create frost pockets by trapping cold air on the uphill or shady side. If these are arranged to deflect the flow of cold air around gardens and outdoor living areas, they provide shelter and protection. Buildings, automobiles, large expanses of concrete, and other heat-absorbing surfaces all contribute to making cities and towns warmer than outlying areas. Likewise, the warmest areas in the garden are usually those beside paved surfaces such as sidewalks, driveways, patios, and sunny south and west walls. Not only do these surfaces reflect some of the sun's heat and light, but they also store heat during daylight hours and radiate it back to the atmosphere at night. Dark surfaces absorb more heat than light-colored ones.

Each side of a building has its own microclimate, which strongly influences plant growth. The cool, shaded, north side is best for cold-tolerant plants and those that do not grow well in full sunlight. A wall that faces south receives maximum sunlight throughout the year; plants that tolerate greater heat and brilliant sunlight do well here. Both east- and west-facing walls are exposed to a half-day of sun, but higher afternoon temperatures create a hotter microclimate against the west wall.

TREE SELECTION LISTS

When you are searching for the right tree to suit a particular location, need, or problem area, organized lists can be helpful. Use the lists in this chapter to guide you in your selection. Some trees are listed by their attributes or characteristics, and others are listed by their functions. Keep in mind that one tree may fulfill many needs. If you are considering a tree for the patio, for example, also consider it for summer flowers, fall color, and winter form. Although no one tree will fit all categories, a certain kind of tree may have the characteristics that matter most to you.

Think of trees not as single, isolated plantings but as groupings that can solve problems. There are many situations in which trees are very useful. For instance, a row of trees can be used as a screen to create privacy if your home is close to the one next door. When planted against plain and imposing walls, trees can add grace and natural beauty. Trees can hide a fence, or they can be miniaturized and kept in pots or tubs for years, if space is limited. Trees can help out problem sites: Some will withstand flooding, grow along a seacoast, or stand up to harsh city conditions.

Each tree listing that follows includes the most frequently used common name as well as the botanical name. Common names may vary; botanical names do not. Listings are arranged in alphabetical order by botanical name. A range of hardiness zones follows each tree listing and indicates the temperature range in which the tree can be grown. Refer to the map on page 108 for zone boundaries. These zones are listed to guide you, but remember that zoning is, at best, only a generality. Tree performance varies by location. Check with a local nursery or county extension agent to be sure the tree will grow in your area.

Trees for Special Uses

The lists that follow include trees suited to special uses. Note that where an entire genus is listed (the genus name followed by the word *species*) hardiness zones for individual species within that genus may vary. See the "Encyclopedia of Trees" (beginning on page 55) for complete descriptions. Lists included in this chapter cover the following topics.

Trees That Attract Birds
Trees That Can Be Sheared
Trees With Attractive Fruits or Berries
Trees With Color in More Than One Season
Wall Trees
Trees That Tolerate Seashore Conditions
Rugged Trees
Trees That Are Tolerant of Flooding
Trees That Are Pest Free
Trees for Fragrance
Trees That Look Attractive in a Grove
Trees for Screens and Buffers
Trees That Tolerate Urban Conditions
Summer-Flowering Trees
Indoor Trees
Small Garden and Patio Trees
Trees With Excellent Fall Color
Trees With an Attractive Winter Silhouette
Quick-Growing Trees
Trees for Windbreaks

Trees That Attract Birds

Almost all trees attract birds. However, because these trees provide abundant fruit as well as cover, they attract birds in large numbers.

Amelanchier canadensis
Serviceberry — 4, 5

Arbutus species
Madrone — 7–9

Cornus species
Dogwood — 5–9

Crataegus species
Hawthorn — 5–9

Eriobotrya japonica
Loquat — 7–9

Ilex species
Holly — 5–10

Juniperus virginiana
Eastern red cedar — 3–7

Laurus nobilis
Sweet bay — 8–10

Malus species
Crab apple — 2–9

Prunus species
Plums, cherries, cherry-laurels — 4–10

Quercus species
Oak — 3–9

Sorbus species
Mountain ash — 3–7

Trees That Can Be Sheared

Shearing, the cutting back of the entire tree canopy, is the simplest method of reducing the amount of foliage. Although many trees respond poorly to this treatment, the following are some of the trees that can be sheared.

Carpinus betulus
European hornbeam — 4–7

Cedrus species
Cedar — 5–10

× *Cupressocyparis leylandii*
Leyland cypress — 6–10

Cupressus species
Cypress — 7–10

Fagus sylvatica
European beech — 5–7

Ginkgo biloba
Maidenhair tree — 4–9

Ilex species
Holly — 5–10

Juniperus virginiana
Eastern red cedar — 3–7

Laurus nobilis
Sweet bay — 8–10

Ligustrum lucidum
Glossy privet — 8–10

Malus species
Crab apple — 2–9

Olea europaea
Olive — 9, 10

Pittosporum species
Pittosporum — 8–10

Cupressus macrocarpa
(Monterey cypress)

Platanus × *acerifolia*
London plane tree   5–9

Podocarpus macrophyllus
Yew pine   8–10

Pseudotsuga menziesii
Douglas fir   4–9

Thuja species
Arborvitae   3–9

Tsuga canadensis
Canadian eastern hemlock   3–7

Trees With Attractive Fruits Or Berries

Bright colors are not limited to foliage and flowers. Fruits and berries, both edible and inedible, can be just as attractive—and sometimes they last longer.

Amelanchier canadensis
Serviceberry   4, 5

Arbutus species
Madrone   7–9

Top: Arbutus unedo (strawberry tree)
Bottom: Acer palmatum atropurpureum (red Japanese maple)

Chionanthus virginicus
Fringe tree   4–9

Cornus species
Dogwood   5–9

Crataegus species
Hawthorn   5–9

Diospyros species
Persimmon   5–9

Ilex species
Holly   5–10

Koelreuteria paniculata
Goldenrain tree   5–9

Malus species
Crab apple   2–9

Oxydendrum arboreum
Sourwood   5–9

Prunus species
Plums, cherries, cherry-laurels   4–10

Sorbus species
Mountain ash   3–7

Trees With Color in More Than One Season

These trees provide interest over a long period with their flowers, fruits, autumn color, or bark.

Acer palmatum
Japanese maple   6–9

Amelanchier canadensis
Serviceberry   4, 5

Betula species
Birch   2–10

Chionanthus virginicus
Fringe tree   4–9

Cladrastis lutea
Yellowwood   4–9

Cornus species
Dogwood   5–9

Crataegus species
Hawthorn   5–9

Diospyros kaki
Kaki persimmon   7–9

Ilex species
Holly   5–10

Koelreuteria paniculata
Goldenrain tree   5–9

Lagerstroemia indica
Crape myrtle   7–10

Malus species
Crab apple   2–9

Oxydendrum arboreum
Sourwood   5–9

Prunus species
Plums, cherries, cherry-laurels   4–10

Pyrus calleryana
Callery pear   5–9

Stewartia pseudocamellia
Japanese stewartia   6–8

Styrax japonicus
Japanese snowbell   5–8

Wall Trees

The trees on this list have root systems and habits that allow for close planting to walls—ideal for softening the look of a one- to two-story building or for lining a fence.

Acer palmatum Japanese maple	6–9
Betula species Birch	2–10
Calocedrus decurrens Incense cedar	5–10
Carpinus betulus 'Fastigiata' European hornbeam	4–7
Chamaecyparis lawsoniana Lawson cypress	6–9
Crataegus phaenopyrum Washington thorn	5–9
Eucalyptus species Eucalyptus	9, 10
Ilex opaca American holly	5–9
Laurus nobilis Sweet bay	8–10
Malus species Crab apple	2–9
Picea glauca White spruce	3, 4
Podocarpus macrophyllus Yew pine	8–10
Pyrus species Pear	5–10

Trees That Tolerate Seashore Conditions

Use these trees along the seacoast. They will tolerate salt spray and heavy winds. Many will lose their natural habit of growth and become sculpted by the ocean winds.

Acer platanoides Norway maple	4–9
Acer rubrum Red maple	3–7
Arbutus species Madrone	7–9
Carpinus betulus European hornbeam	4–7
Cupressus macrocarpa Monterey cypress	8–10
Erythrina species Coral tree	10
Eucalyptus species Eucalyptus	9, 10
Juniperus virginiana Eastern red cedar	3–7
Koelreuteria paniculata Goldenrain tree	5–9
Nyssa sylvatica Black tupelo	4–9

Top: Cupressus macrocarpa (Monterey cypress)
Bottom: Podocarpus macrophyllus (yew pine)

Pinus thunbergiana Japanese black pine	5–8
Platanus × *acerifolia* London plane tree	5–9
Populus nigra 'Italica' Lombardy poplar	2–6
Salix alba var. *tristis* Golden weeping willow	2–9
Ulmus parvifolia Chinese elm	5–9

Rugged Trees

These trees will grow under adverse conditions, often where other species have failed.

Acacia melanoxylon Blackwood acacia	9, 10
Acer buergeranum Trident maple	6–9
Carya illinoinensis Pecan	6–9

Gleditsia triacanthos var. *inermis* (thornless common honeylocust)

Taxodium distichum (bald cypress)

Casuarina cunninghamiana Beefwood	9, 10
Celtis occidentalis Common hackberry	5–8
Eucalyptus species Eucalyptus	9, 10
Fraxinus species Ash	3–10
Ginkgo biloba Maidenhair tree	4–9
Gleditsia triacanthos var. *inermis* Thornless common honeylocust	5–9
Juniperus virginiana Eastern red cedar	3–7
Malus species Crab apple	2–9
Metasequoia glyptostroboides Dawn redwood	5–8
Platanus × *acerifolia* London plane tree	5–9
Populus species Poplar	2–10
Rhus lancea African sumac	8–10
Robinia pseudoacacia Black locust	4–9
Salix species Willow	2–9
Taxodium distichum Bald cypress	5–10
Ulmus parvifolia Chinese elm	5–9

Trees That Are Tolerant Of Flooding

Plant flood-tolerant trees in landscapes where soils may be excessively wet, such as low-lying, poorly drained areas. Flood-tolerant trees are also suited to shoreline plantings that must withstand periodic flooding. The trees listed here can often survive in standing water for 50 days or more.

Acer saccharinum Silver maple	3–7
Betula nigra River birch	5–10
Celtis occidentalis Common hackberry	5–8
Diospyros virginiana American persimmon	5–9
Fraxinus pennsylvanica Green ash	3–8
Gleditsia triacanthos var. *inermis* Thornless common honeylocust	5–9
Liquidambar styraciflua American sweet gum	5–10
Metasequoia glyptostroboides Dawn redwood	5–8
Nyssa sylvatica Black tupelo	4–9
Platanus × *acerifolia* London plane tree	5–9
Populus species Poplar	2–10
Quercus phellos Willow oak	6–9
Salix species Willow	2–9
Taxodium distichum Bald cypress	5–10

Left: Metasequoia glyptostroboides (dawn redwood)
Right: Prunus serrulata 'Mt. Fuji' (Japanese flowering cherry)

Trees That Are Pest Free

"Pest free" is a relative term, depending on locality. These trees are usually pest free where well adapted but may be vulnerable to insect invasion when planted in a place other than their preferred environment.

Acer buergeranum Trident maple	6–9
Cedrus species Cedar	5–10
Celtis species Hackberry	5–9
Cercidiphyllum japonicum Katsura	4–8
Chionanthus virginicus Fringe tree	4–9
Eucalyptus species Eucalyptus	9, 10
Ginkgo biloba Maidenhair tree	4–9
Koelreuteria paniculata Goldenrain tree	5–9
Laurus nobilis Sweet bay	8–10
Liquidambar styraciflua American sweet gum	5–10
Magnolia species Magnolia	4–9
Metasequoia glyptostroboides Dawn redwood	5–8
Nyssa sylvatica Black tupelo	4–9
Olea europaea Olive	9, 10
Ostrya virginiana American hop hornbeam	4–9
Phellodendron amurense Amur corktree	4–7
Pistacia chinensis Chinese pistachio	6–10
Sophora japonica Japanese pagoda tree	5–10
Stewartia species Stewartia	6–8
Taxodium distichum Bald cypress	5–10
Zelkova serrata Japanese zelkova	5–9

Trees for Fragrance

Although the flowers of some trees are inconspicuous, their presence in the garden is a decided pleasure.

Acer ginnala Amur maple	3–8
Chionanthus virginicus Fringe tree	4–9
Cladrastis lutea Yellowwood	4–9
Halesia carolina Carolina silver bell	5–9
Magnolia species Magnolia	4–9
Malus species Crab apple	2–9
Oxydendrum arboreum Sourwood	5–9
Prunus species Plums, cherries, cherry-laurels	4–10
Robinia pseudoacacia Black locust	4–9
Sophora japonica Japanese pagoda tree	5–10
Styrax japonicus Japanese snowbell	5–8
Syringa reticulata Japanese lilac tree	4–7
Tilia cordata Littleleaf linden	4–9

Top: Quercus agrifolia
(coast live oak)
*Bottom: Pinus
thunbergiana*
(Japanese black pine)

Trees That Look Attractive In a Grove

A grove is a group of trees in an open area, usually made up of one type of tree. A grove can provide pleasure when seen from a distance, as well as being a tranquil retreat.

Betula species Birch	2–10
Fagus sylvatica European beech	5–7
Metasequoia glyptostroboides Dawn redwood	5–8
Pinus species Pine	2–10
Populus species Poplar	2–10
Quercus species Oak	3–9
Taxodium distichum Bald cypress	5–10
Tsuga species Hemlock	3–7

Trees for Screens and Buffers

These trees are useful for hiding unattractive areas or for screening adjoining properties.

Abies species Fir	4–8
Acacia melanoxylon Blackwood acacia	9, 10
Calocedrus decurrens Incense cedar	5–10
Cedrus deodara Deodar cedar	7–10
Chamaecyparis obtusa Hinoki false-cypress	5–8
Cupressus species Cypress	7–10
Eucalyptus species Eucalyptus	9, 10
Ilex species Holly	5–10
Juniperus species Juniper	3–10
Laurus nobilis Sweet bay	8–10
Ligustrum lucidum Glossy privet	8–10
Olea europaea Olive	9, 10
Picea species Spruce	3–9
Pinus species Pine	2–10
Populus species Poplar	2–10
Prunus species Plums, cherries, cherry-laurels	4–10
Sequoia sempervirens Coast redwood	7–9
Thuja occidentalis American arborvitae	3–9
Thuja plicata Western red cedar	5–8
Tsuga canadensis Canadian hemlock	3–7

Trees That Tolerate Urban Conditions

These trees vary in local adaptation, but all tolerate city conditions such as air pollution, reflected heat, and limited open soil surface for air and water penetration.

Acacia melanoxylon Blackwood acacia	9, 10
Acer rubrum Red maple	3–7
Aesculus × carnea Red horsechestnut	4–8

Carpinus betulus European hornbeam	4–7
Casuarina cunninghamiana Beefwood	9, 10
Catalpa species Catalpa	5–9
Celtis occidentalis Common hackberry	5–8
Chionanthus virginicus Fringe tree	4–9
Cotinus coggygria Smoke tree	5–9
Crataegus species Hawthorn	5–9
Eucalyptus species Eucalyptus	9, 10
Fraxinus species Ash	3–10
Ginkgo biloba Maidenhair tree	4–9
Gleditsia triacanthos var. *inermis* Thornless common honeylocust	5–9
Ilex opaca American holly	5–9
Koelreuteria paniculata Goldenrain tree	5–9
Laurus nobilis Sweet bay	8–10
Malus species Crab apple	2–9
Metasequoia glyptostroboides Dawn redwood	5–8
Nyssa sylvatica Black tupelo	4–9
Ostrya virginiana American hop hornbeam	4–9
Phellodendron amurense Amur corktree	4–7
Pinus nigra Austrian pine	4–8
Pinus sylvestris Scotch pine	3–8
Pinus thunbergiana Japanese black pine	5–8
Pistacia chinensis Chinese pistachio	6–10
Platanus × *acerifolia* London plane tree	5–9
Pyrus calleryana Callery pear	5–9
Quercus species Oak	3–9
Robinia pseudoacacia Black locust	4–9
Sophora japonica Japanese pagoda tree	5–10
Taxodium distichum Bald cypress	5–10
Tilia cordata Littleleaf linden	4–9
Ulmus parvifolia Chinese elm	5–9
Zelkova serrata Japanese zelkova	5–9

Pyrus calleryana
(callery pear)

Top: Araucaria heterophylla (Norfolk Island pine)
Bottom: Jacaranda acutifolia (jacaranda)

Summer-Flowering Trees

Many trees are colorful long after the first spring blooms are over. Here are some trees with beautiful summer flowers.

Albizia julibrissin Silk tree	7–10
Catalpa species Catalpa	5–9
Cladrastis lutea Yellowwood	4–9
Cornus kousa Kousa dogwood	5–9
Cotinus coggygria Smoke tree	5–9
Crataegus phaenopyrum Washington thorn	5–9
Erythrina species Coral tree	10
Jacaranda acutifolia Jacaranda	10
Koelreuteria paniculata Goldenrain tree	5–9
Lagerstroemia indica Crape myrtle	7–10
Liriodendron tulipifera Tulip tree	5–9
Magnolia grandiflora Southern magnolia	7–9
Oxydendrum arboreum Sourwood	5–9
Rhus chinensis 'September Beauty' September Beauty Chinese sumac	4–8
Sophora japonica Japanese pagoda tree	5–10
Stewartia species Stewartia	6–8
Styrax japonicus Japanese snowbell	5–8
Syringa reticulata Japanese lilac tree	4–7
Vitex agnus-castus Chaste tree	7–10

Indoor Trees

Here are a few outdoor trees suitable for common indoor conditions. Note that these are indoor trees, so no hardiness zones are given.

Araucaria heterophylla
Norfolk Island pine

Laurus nobilis
Sweet bay

Ligustrum lucidum
Glossy privet

Pittosporum species
Pittosporum

Podocarpus macrophyllus
Yew pine

Left: Halesia carolina
(Carolina silver bell)
Right: Ginkgo biloba
(maidenhair tree)

Small Garden and Patio Trees

These are smaller trees that provide shade and seasonal show while accommodating and enhancing patio and garden activities.

Acer palmatum Japanese maple	6–9
Amelanchier canadensis Serviceberry	4, 5
Bauhinia species Orchid tree	7–10
Carpinus betulus European hornbeam	4–7
Cercis canadensis Eastern redbud	2–8
Chionanthus virginicus Fringe tree	4–9
Cornus florida Flowering dogwood	5–9
Cornus kousa Japanese dogwood	5–9
Cotinus coggygria Smoke tree	5–9
Crataegus species Hawthorn	4–9
Eriobotrya japonica Loquat	7–9
Halesia carolina Carolina silver bell	5–9
Koelreuteria paniculata Goldenrain tree	5–9
Lagerstroemia indica Crape myrtle	7–10
Magnolia stellata Star magnolia	5–9
Magnolia virginiana Sweetbay magnolia	5–9
Malus species Crab apple	2–9

Ostrya virginiana American hop hornbeam	4–9
Oxydendrum arboreum Sourwood	5–9
Pistachia chinensis Chinese pistachio	6–10
Prunus species Plums, cherries, cherry-laurels	4–10
Pyrus kawakamii Evergreen pear	8–10
Stewartia koreana Korean stewartia	6–8
Styrax japonicus Japanese snowbell	5–8
Syringa reticulata Japanese lilac tree	4–7

Trees With Excellent Fall Color

In many parts of the country, trees offer a breathtaking kaleidoscope of fall color. Here are trees known for their colorful autumn foliage.

Acer species Maple	3–9
Amelanchier canadensis Serviceberry	4, 5
Betula species Birch	2–10
Cercidiphyllum japonicum Katsura	4–8
Cornus species Dogwood	5–9
Cotinus coggygria Smoke tree	5–9
Diospyros virginiana American common persimmon	5–9
Fraxinus species Ash	3–10

*Cercidiphyllum
japonicum* (katsura)

Ginkgo biloba Maidenhair tree	4-9
Lagerstroemia indica Crape myrtle	7-10
Larix kaempferi Japanese larch	5-8
Liquidambar styraciflua American sweet gum	5-10
Liriodendron tulipifera Tulip tree	5-9
Nyssa sylvatica Black tupelo	4-9
Oxydendrum arboreum Sourwood	5-9
Parrotia persica Persian parrotia	6-8
Pistacia chinensis Chinese pistachio	6-10
Populus species Poplar	2-10
Pyrus calleryana Callery pear	5-9
Quercus coccinea Scarlet oak	4-9
Sapium japonicum Japanese sapium	6-8
Sapium sebiferum Chinese tallow tree	8-10
Sassafras albidum Sassafras	5-9
Zelkova serrata Japanese zelkova	5-9

Trees With an Attractive Winter Silhouette

When leafless, these trees provide a handsome outline against the open sky or next to a background of evergreens. They are winter's visual delights.

Acer species Maple	3-9
Alnus species Alder	3-7
Betula nigra River birch	5-10
Carpinus betulus European hornbeam	4-7
Cercidiphyllum japonicum Katsura	4-8
Cladrastis lutea Yellowwood	4-9
Cornus florida Flowering dogwood	5-9
Fagus sylvatica European beech	5-7
Ginkgo biloba Maidenhair tree	4-9
Gleditsia triacanthos var. *inermis* Thornless common honeylocust	5-9
Ilex opaca American holly	5-9
Lagerstroemia indica Crape myrtle	7-10
Liquidambar styraciflua American sweet gum	5-10

Left: Populus alba
(white poplar)
Right: Populus nigra
'Italica' (Lombardy
poplar)

Liriodendron tulipifera Tulip tree	5-9
Magnolia species Magnolia	4-9
Malus species Crab apple	2-9
Metasequoia glyptostroboides Dawn redwood	5-8
Nyssa sylvatica Black tupelo	4-9
Phellodendron amurense Amur corktree	4-7
Pistacia chinensis Chinese pistachio	6-10
Platanus × acerifolia London plane tree	5-9
Populus species Poplar	2-10
Quercus alba White oak	4-9
Salix species Willow	2-9
Stewartia koreana Korean stewartia	6-8
Ulmus parvifolia Chinese elm	5-9
Zelkova serrata Japanese zelkova	5-9

Quick-Growing Trees

These trees supply quick landscape effect. Some may be considered "weed trees," but they can be interplanted with "desirables" and removed as the slower trees reach functional size.

Acacia species Acacia	9, 10
Acer saccharinum Silver maple	3-7
Albizia julibrissin Silk tree	7-10
Alnus species Alder	3-7

Casuarina cunninghamiana Beefwood	9, 10
Catalpa species Catalpa	5-9
Eucalyptus species Eucalyptus	9, 10
Paulownia tomentosa Empress tree	6-9
Populus species Poplar	2-10
Robinia pseudoacacia Black locust	4-9
Salix species Willow	2-9
Sapium sebiferum Chinese tallow tree	8-10
Ulmus parvifolia Chinese elm	5-9

Trees for Windbreaks

Wind can be a major menace, especially in winter. It breaks snow-laden branches, dries exposed branches and foliage, and increases existing cold (the windchill factor). A permanent windbreak can effectively mitigate the effects of strong winds. Use hardy and structurally sound trees for windbreaks.

Celtis occidentalis Common hackberry	5-8
Chamaecyparis pisifera Sawara false-cypress	4-8
Juniperus virginiana Eastern red cedar	3-7
Picea abies Norway spruce	3-8
Pinus strobus White pine	2-8
Populus nigra 'Italica' Lombardy poplar	2-6
Rhamnus alaternus Italian buckthorn	7-9

Encyclopedia of Trees

This encyclopedia provides specific information on many different trees. Use it to select trees appropriate for your needs or as a guide to help you identify and expand your knowledge about the trees around you.

Only a fraction of the innumerable species and varieties of trees are presented in this encyclopedia. The trees described here were chosen for their outstanding qualities, usefulness, availability, and frequency in the landscape across the United States and southern Canada.

The trees are listed alphabetically by botanical name. Where there is more than one entry within a given genus, a description of the genus itself is included. If only one species within a genus is listed, no genus introduction is provided. If you do not know the botanical name for the tree you are interested in, look up the common name in the index on pages 109 to 112.

The botanical name is given in the following way: The first word is the genus, which is always capitalized, for example, *Gleditsia*. The second word refers to the specific type, that is, the species, and is not capitalized, as in *Gleditsia triacanthos*. If there is a varietal name (the name for a group of plants that differs slightly from the specific type and occurs in the wild), it follows the genus and species and is written after the abbreviation for the word *variety* (var.), for example, *Gleditsia triacanthos* var. *inermis*. (Here *inermis* refers to the thornless variety.)

Trees selected for special form and growth characteristics are propagated vegetatively, that is, by grafting, budding, or stem cuttings

Bright red autumn leaves carpet the area around this Japanese maple.

Top: The art of bonsai,
introduced from China
to Japan in the
thirteenth century, is
still practiced today.
Bottom: This live oak
tree frames the garden
and creates an
impressive outline
against the sky.

rather than by seed. Such trees are called cultivars, which is short for cultivated varieties.
The names of cultivars are always capitalized
and in single quotes and follow the species
name or variety, for example, *Gleditsia
triacanthos* var. *inermis* 'Sunburst'.

Hortus Third is the usual reference for
botanical nomenclature and is the one used in
this encyclopedia. If any of the entries are
known by another botanical name, it follows
the preferred name and is in parentheses.

The common name or names for each entry
appear below the botanical name. Information
on the type of tree, whether evergreen or deciduous, follows the common name. The zones in
which the particular tree grows, the country or
region of its origin, and finally its growth habit
are also listed.

The terms describing growth habit are relative. Rapid or fast growing, for example, may
have different meanings in different locales. In
this book rapid or fast growing means annual
growth of more than 2 feet in height. Moderate
growing indicates growth of 1 to 2 feet in
height per year, and slow growing means
growth of less than 1 foot in height per year.

Height is also relative. It depends on soil,
water, climate, and other environmental fac-
tors. A Douglas fir that matures at 200 feet in
an Oregon forest will attain only 20 feet at maturity in the Chisos Mountains of the Bend
country of Texas. Also, if a particular tree
stands among other trees, it may have no other
way to grow except up. Given here is the height
the tree should reach in 50 or 60 years under
average cultivated conditions if it were standing alone, rather than in a forest or grove.

Abies concolor (white fir)

Acacia baileyana (bailey acacia, cootamundra-wattle)

Acacia melanoxylon (blackwood acacia)

ABIES
FIR

The many species of fir available vary according to location. All form perfectly pyramidal trees that need a good deal of room to develop.

Firs are best used in open lawns, parks, or golf courses and grow well in moist, well-drained, nonalkaline soils protected from high winds. They are a poor choice for hot, dry areas, but grow well in cool-climate conifer forests where they may reach up to 200 feet.

Abies concolor
White fir

Needled evergreen
Zones 4–8
Native to the western United States
Moderate growing to 80–100 feet; can grow to 200 feet

The white fir is more tolerant of heat, drought, and city conditions than other fir species. The needles are blue-green or gray-green and about 2 inches long. Horizontal branches hold upright, cylindrical cones that cluster on upper branches. Younger trees have smooth, gray bark and make fragrant container Christmas trees.

Abies nordmanniana
Nordmann fir

Needled evergreen
Zones 5–8
Native to Asia Minor and the Mediterranean
Slow to moderate growing to 55–65 feet

Dark, shiny, green needles with silver undersides densely cover the horizontal branches of this tree. Like *Abies concolor,* it can be grown in a container for several years and makes an excellent Christmas tree. It is relatively heat tolerant.

Abies procera
Noble fir

Needled evergreen
Zones 5–7
Native to the northwestern United States
Fast growing to 100–150 feet

One of the most handsome of all firs, the noble fir forms a narrow tree with a stiff branching habit and blue-green foliage closely arranged on the twigs. It needs a cool climate in order to thrive.

ACACIA
ACACIA

This large group of evergreen or deciduous trees is native to the tropics and other warm regions of the world. It has adapted well to California and Arizona landscapes and is known for its typically bright yellow flowers.

The acacias exhibit great variation in their foliage: The leaves of some species are feathery and finely divided; others are long and narrow. In general, the acacias are fast growing (up to 20 feet in 3 years) but short-lived (20 to 30 years).

Acacia baileyana
Bailey acacia, cootamundra-wattle

Evergreen
Zones 9, 10
Native to Australia
Fast growing to 20 feet tall and 20 feet wide

The daffodil-yellow flowers for which this acacia is famous bloom profusely in January and February, even on young trees. A mature tree in full bloom is an unforgettable sight. The mass of bright color eclipses the fine, blue-gray, fernlike foliage completely. This species grows best in dry, well-drained soils but is tough enough to stand less optimal conditions. *Acacia baileyana* 'Purpurea' is a beautiful variety with purple new growth.

Acacia melanoxylon
Blackwood acacia

Evergreen
Zones 9, 10
Native to Australia
Fast growing to 40 feet or more; upright, with a broad, pyramidal head

Acer griseum (paperbark maple)

Acer palmatum (Japanese maple)

The blackwood acacia has dark green leaves that are 2 to 4 inches long and inconspicuous, pale yellow flowers. This is a tree that will stand difficult conditions. Use it as a fast-growing windbreak or screen or as erosion control. The root system can break up pavement, so do not plant where this could be a problem.

ACER
MAPLE

Among the 90 species of maples there is a great variety in size, foliage, and color. In size, they range from 100-foot giants to low shrubs. The leaves vary from broad 12-inch specimens to palmate ribbons 3 inches wide. White, yellow, many shades of green, pink, and maroon-red are found in the summer foliage, and the fall colors of yellow, orange, and red are legendary.

The constant features that help to identify maples are the winged seeds, called samaras, and the opposite arrangement of the leaves on the branches and the branches on the trunk.

Verticillium wilt can be a problem, and so can aphids and the honeydew they secrete. Also troublesome to some gardeners is the fertility of some species and cultivars—especially as wind disperses the samaras or winged seeds over a wide area.

Acer buergeranum
Trident maple

Deciduous
Zones 6–9
Native to Japan and China
Grows to 50 feet with a narrow, rounded head

The sharply three-pointed leaves explain the common name of this round-headed maple. The 3-inch leaves are glossy green, turning yellow to red in the fall. This species often grows with multiple stems and low branches, but it can be trained to a single stem and pruned for head clearance. It is used widely as an urban street tree in Japan.

Acer ginnala
Amur maple

Deciduous
Zones 3–8
Native to northeastern Asia
Broad oval or globe shape; 20 feet tall and 20 feet wide

This tree is tolerant of both cold and wind and usually has multiple stems. Its fragrant flowers are a novelty among maples. Summer color is provided by the bright red fruit; later, the foliage also turns bright red. It is sometimes used as a substitute for the Japanese maple in cold regions.

Acer griseum
Paperbark maple

Deciduous
Zones 5–7
Native to western China
Slow growing to 20–30 feet tall and about half as wide with a rounded, rather open habit

Red-brown peeling bark gives this maple outstanding year-round interest. Its olive to gray-green compound leaves have three coarsely toothed leaflets. The foliage is pendant with an orange-brown to scarlet autumn color.

Paperbark maple trees need little pruning; low limbs can be removed to show off the trunk better. This species does best in full sun but tolerates moderate shade. It grows in any soil, but extreme alkalinity can cause chlorosis. Its flowers are small and sulfur yellow in early spring, and its double-winged dry seed capsule is gray-green fading to light brown.

Acer palmatum
Japanese maple

Deciduous
Zones 6–9
Native to China and Japan
Slow-growing, small tree to 20 feet tall and 20 feet wide

This is a highly variable species that can even be grown in a low, multistemmed, spreading mound. Its leaves are 2 to 4 inches long, and each has five to nine toothed lobes. Leaf color may be solid or variegated. Solids range from yellow-green to maroon-red; varigated forms are white and pink.

Acer platanoides (Norway maple)

Acer rubrum (red maple, swamp maple)

Leaf color develops best in full sun, but it may be necessary to grow the species in light shade if hot, dry winds are a problem. Descriptions of some of the best of the cultivars follow.

'Atropurpureum' is one of the hardiest of the Japanese maples, with five-lobed leaves that remain red all summer.

'Osakazuki' has seven-lobed green leaves that turn bright red in the fall.

'Dissectum' has finely divided cut-leaf forms available with green or red leaves.

'Sangokaku' is a green-leafed type with coral bark that is very attractive in a winter landscape.

Acer platanoides

Norway maple

Deciduous
Zones 4–9
Native to western Asia
Grows to 40–50 feet tall and 65–75 feet wide

More than 20 varieties of this rugged species have been recorded, some with varied growth form, others with differing foliage colors. This tree creates very dense shade, and its yellow flowers produce a colorful display. The vigorous root system and thick leaf canopy make it difficult to grow grass or other plants around the tree base. Seedlings can be invasive, and in some areas this tree is considered an aggressive weed.

Among the selected forms are the following.

'Cleveland' is quite columnar as a young tree, eventually forming a broad oval, 50 feet tall and 25 to 30 feet wide. The dark green leaves are prone to leaf scorch in dry, hot weather. They turn yellow in fall.

'Crimson King' is probably the best-known variety of Norway maple. The leaves remain maroon-red throughout the season. Growth is somewhat slower than the green-leafed types, forming a tree 35 to 40 feet tall and 50 feet wide.

'Drummondii', with white-green leaves, gives a cool appearance on a hot day, although the white areas are apt to burn and the leaves often revert to the green form. It will form a tree 40 to 50 feet tall and 35 to 45 feet wide.

'Emerald Queen' is a fast-growing cultivar with an upright, spreading form. It can be expected to grow 50 feet tall and 50 feet wide. It is one of the best cultivars for yellow fall colors.

'Summer Shade' is a fast-growing selection that grows to 45 to 50 feet with a 60- to 70-foot spread. The heavily textured leaves of this cultivar are heat resistant.

Acer rubrum

Red maple, swamp maple

Deciduous
Zones 3–7
Native to eastern North America
Fast growing to a height of 50–60 feet tall and 40–60 feet wide; symmetrical, spreading, pyramidal

This is a fast-growing species with relatively small leaves and somewhat stronger wood than the silver maple (see page 60). The shade it produces is not as dense as that of the other large maples. It has attractive, small, red flowers in early spring. This species grows in wet as well as normal soil and develops fall color under both conditions.

Many selections have been developed, both for growth form and fall color.

'Autumn Flame' forms a round-headed tree 30 to 40 feet tall and as wide. This selection consistently turns orange-red one to two weeks before the others. Leaf fall is also one to two weeks earlier.

'Bowhall' has a narrow, pyramidal form 45 feet tall and 15 feet wide. It has good fall color and is useful near buildings and streets where other trees with wider-spreading limbs could be hazardous.

'Red Sunset' is a broad, pyramidal tree, 50 to 60 feet tall and 30 to 40 feet wide. This species' heavy production of red flowers in spring and red fall foliage make it one of the most colorful selections.

'October Glory' has a broad, pyramidal form and grows 50

Acer saccharinum (silver maple, soft maple)

Acer saccharum (sugar maple, rock maple)

Aesculus × carnea
(red horsechestnut)

to 60 feet tall and 30 to 40 feet wide. It has particularly lustrous leaves, which turn brilliant red late in the fall.

Acer saccharinum
Silver maple, soft maple

Deciduous
Zones 3–7
Native to eastern North America
Fast growing to 100 feet with a broad, open crown 70 feet wide

Heat and dryness have a less adverse effect on this species than on other maples, so it is used for quick shade where other trees fail. Limb breakage in wind or storms is a serious problem. Because of this, some cities have prohibited the planting of the silver maple as a street tree. Check local ordinances before doing so. This tree is best planted away from buildings and utility wires. The foliage of the silver maple does not change color in the fall.

Acer saccharum
Sugar maple, rock maple

Deciduous
Zones 3–7
Native to eastern North America
Fast growing to 80–100 feet tall and 60–80 feet wide

This maple supplies much of the fall color in New England. It is the source of maple syrup and lumber for maple furniture. It is a relatively hardy tree but does not grow well in the city or in hot, dry conditions. It is more susceptible to damage from soil compaction and salt spray than most maples.

The following are several of the best cultivars of this species.

'Newton Sentry' develops a central leader and a narrow, columnar form.

'Temple's Upright' does not have a central leader but does maintain a columnar form.

'Green Mountain' has the typical broad, oval shape of the species, but its dark green leaves are more resistant to adverse conditions.

'Bonfire' is a vigorous, heat-resistant selection with bright red autumn color.

AESCULUS
HORSECHESTNUT, BUCKEYE

This genus of deciduous trees includes species that are pyramidal or elliptical when young, but all are round headed when mature. They are known for their shiny, inedible fruits and their candlelike flower panicles. The leaves of some species turn yellow in the fall. *Aesculus* grow best in full sun to light shade and in neutral to slightly acid soil.

Aesculus × carnea
Red horsechestnut

Deciduous
Zones 4–8
A hybrid of *A. hippocastanum* (native to southern Europe) and *A. pavia* (native to the southeastern United States)
Slow to moderate growing to 30–50 feet tall and 30 feet

wide; pyramidal when young, erect with round crown when mature

This spectacular flowering tree is at its best in midspring when it bears upright 8- to 10-inch-long, red to pink flower spikes. Its five-fingered leaves are light to dark bright green and tropical looking. It is a very manageable garden, street, or park tree that casts dense shade. Because it is subject to leaf scorch in hot, dry winds, this tree is best grown in areas with cool, moist summers and in protected locations.

'Briotii' is a cultivar that has bright red flowers in large spikes up to 9 inches long.

Aesculus octandra
Yellow buckeye, sweet buckeye

Deciduous
Zones 5–8
Native to the southeastern United States
Fast growing in upright, oval form; 60–70 feet tall and 40–50 feet wide

This species has lovely yellow, candlelike flower clusters that

Albizia julibrissin (silk tree, mimosa)

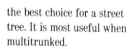

Alnus glutinosa (common alder, black alder, European alder)

bloom in late spring. Its foliage is more handsome than that of other species and has a beautiful orange-yellow autumn color. Its 2-inch-long fruits are oval; its bark a mottled gray and brown. This species is highly resistant to the leaf blotch that often defoliates other species.

This tree grows best in full sun but tolerates light shade. It does not do well in excessively alkaline or dry soils.

Agonis flexuosa
Peppermint tree, Australian willow myrtle

Evergreen
Zones 9, 10
Native to southwestern Australia
Moderate to fast growing to 25–30 feet tall and at least as wide; weeping branches in a spreading, irregular pattern

This small evergreen tree derives its name from the smell of the crushed leaves. The pliable wood, drooping branches, and long, thin, willowlike leaves make this an attractive, light, and airy tree. It has

white flowers that bloom in early summer, new growth tinged coppery red, and interesting bark that sheds with age.

This species makes a good lawn, patio, or tub tree. It is drought and heat tolerant, virtually pest free, and can be espaliered.

Albizia julibrissin
Silk tree, mimosa

Deciduous
Zones 7–10
Native to Asia from Iran through Japan
Fast growing to 25–40 feet tall and greater in width; arching branches form an umbrellalike canopy

This tree is beautiful in summer, when the showy pink, powder-puff-like flowers are held above the fernlike, almost feathery, light green leaves. The light-sensitive foliage folds at night.

The silk tree can be used in a variety of ways, depending on how it's pruned, but because of its many flowers and relatively short life it is not

the best choice for a street tree. It is most useful when multitrunked.

It does well as a lawn tree or in a container but must have plenty of heat and prefers alkaline soil. Its flowers are clustered together and most attractive if seen from above.

This species suffers from wilt and other problems, including weak wood and twig girdlers. Prune wide-spreading branches to help relieve weight that could cause them to break. This tree is considered invasive in some areas, as it seeds prolifically.

Among the cultivars are 'Rosea', which has rich pink flowers and is the hardiest form. 'Charlotte' and 'Tryon' are both wilt resistant, an important consideration in the Northeast, the South, and especially the Midwest.

ALNUS
ALDER

This group of 30 fast-growing, deciduous trees and shrubs is especially useful for damp, difficult areas. This species

has no decorative fruit or autumn color, but flower catkins hang all winter for interest. Some alders are short-lived, others quite long-lived. Some are prone to insect damage, especially from the tent caterpillar. Alders are recommended only for wet or swampy situations where better ornamentals will not survive. They are also useful in sterile, poorly aerated soils, such as those often found in urban areas.

Alnus glutinosa
Common alder, black alder, European alder

Deciduous
Zones 3–7
Native to Europe; naturalized in some parts of the United States
Fast growing to 40–60 feet tall and 20–40 feet wide

This is a valuable tree for wet areas in the East. It will even grow under water, and it does well in poor soils. It will survive adverse city conditions and should be more widely planted in urban sites.

Araucaria heterophylla (Norfolk Island pine)

Arbutus menziesii (madrone, madrona)

Alnus oregona (A. rubra)
Red alder

Deciduous
Zones 4–7
Native to western North America
Fast growing to 40–70 feet with a slender, pyramidal habit

Considered a weed tree by some, this is the most common alder along the Pacific Northwest coast. It thrives in low sites with damp soil and grows rapidly enough to be a commercial source of firewood.

Alnus rhombifolia
White alder

Deciduous
Zones 4–7
Native to the northwestern United States and Canada
Fast growing to 60–70 feet tall and about two thirds as wide; upright, irregular form; gracefully pendant branch tips

This tree is useful as a quick-growing screen and does well in poorly drained soils. Its leaves are dark green above, paler beneath. In late winter the catkins will give a purple tinge to a grove of white alder.

Amelanchier canadensis
Serviceberry, shadblow, shadbush, juneberry

Deciduous
Zones 4, 5
Native to Canada and to the northern and midwestern United States
Moderate growing to 20–40 feet; often multistemmed with an upright, twiggy form

Serviceberry is one of the earliest trees to flower in the East. The snow white blossoms appear just after the flowers of the cornelian-cherries and dogwoods but before the eastern redbud. This durable tree also displays beautiful autumn color and has attractive, smooth, silver gray bark.

Araucaria heterophylla
Norfolk Island pine

Needled evergreen
Zone 10
Native to Norfolk Island (1,000 miles east of Australia)

Moderate growing to 60–70 feet tall and half as wide; formal pyramid with symmetrical branching in horizontal tiers

This tree has a softly formal character and grows quite large in the landscape, especially near the coast. It is often used as an indoor container plant, where it may live for many years.

ARBUTUS
MADRONE

These trees are among the most beautiful of the broadleaf evergreens and should be used in more garden situations. Their small white flowers tinged with pink form red fruit that can stay on the tree for months. This species is also characterized by its bark, which is red to cinnamon and peeling on older branches.

Arbutus are good accent trees where falling bark, flowers, and fruit will not matter. They grow best in dry, sandy, and acidic soil and in full sun with some wind protection.

Arbutus menziesii
Madrone, madrona

Evergreen
Zones 7–9
Native to the Pacific Northwest and California
Slow to moderate growing to as high as 80 feet in native stands; usually smaller, to 20–40 feet, with a broad, irregular, round head

The new foliage of this tree is soft and light green to copper in color. Older leaves become leathery and dark green above with gray undersides. Madrone is especially attractive in groves and grows well near the Pacific coast.

Arbutus unedo
Strawberry tree

Evergreen
Zones 7–9
Native to the Mediterranean countries and Ireland
Slow to moderate growing to 10–25 feet tall and equally wide; irregular, rounding habit

This is a shrubby plant that needs pruning to make a well-formed tree. Leaves are dark

Bauhinia blakeana (Hong Kong orchid tree)

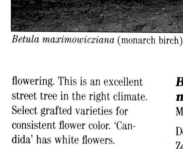

Betula maximowicziana (monarch birch)

green with red stems. Small, white, urn-shaped flowers are followed by fruit that looks like a strawberry but tastes like cotton.

The twisting habit of the tree becomes more attractive with age. The bark is smooth, deep red to brownish red. The tree is best used where it can be looked up into, such as on a patio or lawn. It is adaptable to a range of soil and climate conditions.

BAUHINIA
ORCHID TREE

These distinctive evergreen or deciduous flowering trees are common to southern California, Arizona, Florida, and Hawaii. All orchid trees grow best in a warm, well-drained spot, but suffer in high heat and drought. They are excellent small shade trees.

Bauhinia blakeana
Hong Kong orchid tree

Deciduous
Zones 9, 10
Native to Southeast Asia

Moderate growing to 20 feet; flat-topped, umbrellalike canopy

The Hong Kong orchid tree loses most of its kidney-shaped leaves just long enough to display beautiful pink to purple, orchidlike flowers in late fall to early winter. The flowers are 5 to 6 inches wide, considerably larger than those on most orchid trees.

Bauhinia variegata
Orchid tree

Deciduous
Zones 7-10
Native to India and China
Moderate growing to 20-25 feet with an umbrellalike form; tends to get bushy and multitrunked

This is the *Bauhinia* most common to southern California. Its flower and foliage color vary depending on soil conditions, climate, and exposure. A mild, dry winter produces the most spectacular bloom. Flowers are in shades of white to pink to lavender. The leaves of this tree drop in midwinter and are gone briefly during

flowering. This is an excellent street tree in the right climate. Select grafted varieties for consistent flower color. 'Candida' has white flowers.

BETULA
BIRCH

Birches are valued for the interesting color, texture, and peeling quality of their bark; for their catkins; and for their yellow autumn foliage. Some are so resilient that their slender trunks bend to the ground with ice and snow yet stand back upright after the thaw.

Fairly fast growing, they are good for light shade or for naturalizing at timber edges. But some are prone to damage by aphids, borers, leafminers, and other insects and may be short-lived. They bleed profusely in the spring and should be pruned at other times.

Most species grow best in full sun and moist, cool soil. Selecting the right species for the situation can greatly increase their longevity. Birches grow best in areas with cool summers.

Betula maximowicziana
Monarch birch

Deciduous
Zones 6-10
Native to Japan
Fast growing to 80-100 feet with a wide-spreading, rounded crown

This tree has the largest leaves and catkins of all birches. The older bark is white, and the younger branches are reddish brown. The older, white bark splits and hangs from the tree in shreddy clumps. This large tree must be planted where it has enough room to develop. It is resistant to birch leafminer.

Betula nigra
River birch

Deciduous
Zones 5-10
Native to the eastern United States
Grows to 50-70 feet; pyramidal in habit

This is the most widely adapted of the birches. It is found naturally growing along

Betula pendula (European white birch)

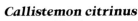

Brachychiton discolor (Queensland lacebark, scrub bottle tree)

riverbanks and on flood plains. The young bark is tan, gradually becoming an attractive, shaggy, chocolate brown.

The river birch requires acidic soil, and its roots must reach moist soil to thrive. This is a good tree to use as a drought indicator, as it is among the first to show moisture stress. It is the most resistant to borer damage.

'Heritage' is a greatly improved cultivar of the river birch. It is a vigorous selection with glossy leaves and heavily exfoliating salmon-white bark.

Betula papyrifera
Paper birch

Deciduous
Zones 3–7
Native to northern North America
Grows to 40–60 feet; open and erect habit

This birch is often called "the lady of the forest." Its white bark brings a lively grace to a group of needled evergreens, and in the winter its white trunk and blue-gray branches provide a bright contrast to

the typical dark brown of other leafless trees.

In general, white birches are trees of the northern regions. Borer injury limits their usefulness unless they are grown in cool and moist areas with well-drained soil.

The natural habit of the birch is to grow in clumps of several trees; therefore, clump planting is suggested for this species.

Betula pendula
European white birch

Deciduous
Zones 2–6
Native to Europe and Asia Minor
Grows to about 60 feet

Rough twigs and white bark with vertical black markings distinguish this birch from others. Older trees often have weeping branches. In this species borer injury can become a serious problem.

The following are common cultivars.

'Fastigiata', the pyramidal European white birch, is

columnar and dense when young. As it matures, it develops its pyramidal shape.

'Gracilis', the cut-leaf European white birch, has finely dissected leaves.

'Tristis' is a tall, graceful tree with slender, pendulous branches.

Brachychiton discolor
Queensland lacebark, scrub bottle tree

Deciduous
Zones 9, 10
Native to Australia
Moderate growing to 40–90 feet; narrow, pyramidal in youth, wider with age

This tree is well suited to warm inland areas. The 6-inch, somewhat maplelike leaves are woolly white beneath and dark green above. They fall just before the tree flowers. Following sudden cold weather, the entire tree may be bare for a period. Blossoms of rose to pink are backed by a short, brown, woolly fuzz, which also distinguishes the 6-inch rust-colored seed pods. This tree is

especially handsome for avenue planting where there is ample sun and heat.

Callistemon citrinus
Lemon-bottlebrush

Evergreen
Zones 8–10
Native to Australia
Fast growing to 20–25 feet; somewhat narrow and round headed

Lemon-bottlebrush blooms the year around, and its leaves are pinkish copper. Both of these attributes contribute to its appeal. This species is very tolerant of both heat and cold and makes a suitable screen or buffer. It can be used espaliered or as a single-trunk specimen.

Calocedrus decurrens
Incense cedar

Needled evergreen
Zones 5–10
Native to the mountains of southern Oregon, California, western Nevada, and Baja California

Callistemon citrinus (lemon-bottlebrush)

Casuarina cunninghamiana (beefwood, river she-oak)

Slow growing in youth, but becomes fast growing, reaching 70–90 feet; dense, columnar form

This species is known for its aromatic, rich green foliage; the fragrance is most apparent in hot weather. The attractive, reddish brown bark is usually concealed by the foliage. This is a handsome tree if given space and is quite useful as a tall hedge and windbreak.

Carpinus betulus
European hornbeam

Deciduous
Zones 4–7
Native to Europe and
Asia Minor
Slow to moderate growing to 30–40 feet tall and 15–25 feet wide; dense, pyramidal shape when young

This is a manageable and attractive tree with dark green, elmlike foliage and smooth, gray bark that becomes fluted with age. Fall color is yellow, and fruit clusters are up to 5 inches long and nutlike in appearance.

'Fastigiata' is the most widely available and trouble-free cultivar. It is one of the best choices for use as a hedge or screen. It is also an excellent street tree and an effective wall tree. It is tolerant of air pollution and does well in a range of soils from dry and rocky to wet but well drained.

Other cultivars available include 'Pyramidalis' and 'Columnaris'.

Carya illinoinensis
Pecan

Deciduous
Zones 6–9
Native to the southeastern United States
Moderate growing to 100 feet and equally wide with a rounded crown

Noted in the South for many years as both a shade tree and a source of food, this tree is now moving into the warm interiors of California. It can also grow in the alkaline soils of arid Arizona and New Mexico but requires supplemental fertilization in such locations. In spite of its susceptibility to

disease, most notably scab, it is a highly sought after species.

Casuarina cunninghamiana
Beefwood, river she-oak

Evergreen
Zones 9, 10
Native to Queensland and New South Wales, Australia
Fast growing to 70 feet; pinelike with spreading drooping branches

Beefwood is a rugged tree, valuable for quick effects. It does well in the Pacific southwest, the Gulf Coast, and in Florida but is considered weedy in some areas. The long, thin branches have leaves that look like needles. The fruit is woody, grayish, and conelike. This is the most graceful member of the Beefwood family.

CATALPA
CATALPA

These large, coarse, fast-growing deciduous trees with big, light green leaves and long beanlike pods do best in parks

and other large spaces. They are useful to homeowners as fast-growing shade trees and may be removed when more choice species grow large and sturdy enough.

Catalpas adapt to a wide variety of conditions and tolerate sun and hot, dry summers. They were once pollarded (see page 27) but this fashion has passed in many areas.

Catalpa bignonioides
Common southern catalpa, Indian-bean, cigar tree

Deciduous
Zones 5–9
Native to the southeastern United States
Fast growing to 35–40 feet and nearly as wide; irregular, broad, rounded crown

When grown in full sun, this tree is covered with white, trumpet-shaped flowers in late spring to early summer. The flowers are spotted with yellow, purple, and brown. The blooms are followed by long, 13- to 18-inch bean pods, which last into winter.

Catalpa speciosa
(northern catalpa)

Cedrus atlantica (atlas cedar)

Cedrus deodara (deodar cedar)

Common catalpa is widely adapted to a range of soils and climates and can tolerate air pollution. It is best used in large areas such as parks. Its dropping of pods, blossoms, leaves, and twigs make this a messy tree.

Catalpa speciosa
Northern catalpa

Deciduous
Zones 5–9
Native to the eastern
United States
Fast growing to 65–75 feet; round headed

Although very similar to *C. bignonioides,* northern catalpa has larger leaves, fewer flowers, and is slightly tougher. It is also larger and should be used only in areas that allow it plenty of space.

CEDRUS
CEDAR

Although many evergreen trees, especially of the cypress family, have been given the common name cedar for their long-lasting, hard, fragrant wood, they are not true cedars.

Cedrus, the true cedars, are conifers and belong to the pine family. There are weeping, golden, blue, columnar, and other forms.

Needles bunched in starlike clusters and an open, spreading habit characterize the true cedars. Cones are woody and rounded. Some are flat on top; others are conical.

Cedars grow best in full sun. When established, true cedars are drought tolerant.

Cedrus atlantica
Atlas cedar

Needled evergreen
Zones 6–9
Native to North Africa
Slow to moderate growing to 50–70 feet tall and 40–60 feet wide; irregular and pyramidal when young; flat topped with a broadly spreading crown at maturity

This species has fine-textured, bluish green needles borne in stiff clusters. This is a fine skyline tree that is drought resistant and excellent in parks, large gardens, or planted along

a boulevard. It is the most popular of the blue conifers. The cultivar 'Glauca' has the richest blue foliage.

Cedrus deodara
Deodar cedar

Needled evergreen
Zones 7–10
Native to the Himalayas
Fast growing to 40–75 feet tall and 20–45 feet wide

This is often considered the most refined, graceful, and soft-textured cedar. Its lower branches sweep to the ground and its upper branches are evenly spaced and well pronounced. The foliage grows in typical cedar clusters but is a soft, light green color. This is the fastest growing of the cedars.

The nodding tip of this tree makes it very recognizable on the skyline. It can be used as a screen, but it is best in parks and in groves. Like other cedars, it needs space to be appreciated but responds to pruning for confinement.

'Kashmir' and 'Shalimar' are cultivars selected for

greater winter hardiness and are useful in zone 6.

Cedrus libani
Cedar of Lebanon

Needled evergreen
Zones 5–7
Native to Asia Minor
Slow growing to 40–70 feet with a large, thick trunk and wide-spreading branches

This cedar is very similar to *C. atlantica* but has dark green foliage and is slower growing and hardier.

CELTIS
HACKBERRY

Hackberries are known for their persistence in adverse situations. They tolerate drought; hot, dry winds; and city conditions. In general, they are pest free.

Celtis australis
European hackberry

Deciduous
Zones 7–9
Native to southern Europe
Moderate growing to 40–70 feet tall and 40–50 feet wide

Celtis occidentalis (common hackberry)

Cercis canadensis (eastern redbud)

European hackberry has dark green leaves with finely toothed edges. The small, edible, dark purple berries it bears are prized by birds. This is an excellent tree for tough, arid regions and should be more widely used in cities. It is valuable as a shade tree, a lawn tree, and as a street tree.

Celtis laevigata
Sugar hackberry, Mississippi hackberry

Deciduous
Zones 6–9
Native to the south central and southeastern United States
Slow to moderate growing to 40–60 feet tall and slightly less wide

This is an upright, spreading tree with dark green foliage that shows little color change in the fall. The bark of the trunk and the larger branches is gray, like that of the American beech. The sugar hackberry is tolerant of a wide range of soil conditions and is less susceptible to the foliage and branch deformation of the common hackberry.

Celtis occidentalis
Common hackberry

Deciduous
Zones 5–8
Native to the central and southeastern United States
Moderate growing to 35–45 feet tall and equally wide; irregular to round headed; spreading, sometimes pendulous branches

The common hackberry has bright green leaves with finely toothed edges and dark red berries that attract birds. It is a valuable shade tree in tough situations but it may suffer from a foliage and branch deformation called witches' broom.

'Prairie Pride' is a witches' broom–resistant cultivar with lustrous, leathery leaves.

Cercidiphyllum japonicum
Katsura

Deciduous
Zones 4–8
Native to Japan
Fast growing to 60 feet tall or higher and often broader than high

When trained as a single-trunked tree (most species are multitrunked), the katsura tree is upright and narrow, but will widen with age. It is broad and spreading, branching upward and outward if left multi-trunked. This is an excellent tree for filtered shade.

The leaves are a lustrous reddish to reddish purple in spring when they first unfold. In the summer the foliage is dark green. The leaves turn scarlet and gold in the fall. Small, dry fruit capsules provide winter ornamentation. Katsura is pest free and grows best in moist soil and light shade. It is intolerant of hot sun, dry winds, drought, and city conditions.

Cercis canadensis
Eastern redbud

Deciduous
Zones 2–8
Native to southeastern Canada and the eastern United States
Moderate growing to 25–35 feet tall and equally wide; irregular, round head with attractive, horizontally tiered branches

Eastern redbud is best known for its magenta-colored pea-shaped flowers that bloom on bare branches in the spring. The blossoms form right on the trunk of this tree. This all-season performer has attractive green, heart-shaped leaves, yellow fall color, and interesting seedpods. In winter, the lovely reddish brown bark shows off the zigzag structure of the branches.

This tree can be grown under almost any conditions: sun, shade, acid soil, alkaline soil, and moist soils. It is, however, susceptible to both wilt and borers, but when stricken, it will often resprout vigorously from the stump.

CHAMAECYPARIS
FALSE-CYPRESS

This is a large group of trees, some of which do well as wall trees, others as lawn specimens. Many are especially useful as screens or tall hedges. When young, they do well in tubs or other containers. The false-cypresses are adapted to cool coastal conditions. They can take moist heat but must

Chamaecyparis lawsoniana (Lawson cypress, Port Orford cedar)

Chamaecyparis nootkatensis (Alaska cedar)

be protected from hot, dry winds. They grow best in moist, well-drained soil. Dwarf forms of this genus are most widely cultivated.

Chamaecyparis lawsoniana
Lawson cypress,
Port Orford cedar

Needled evergreen
Zones 6–9
Native to southwestern Oregon and northwestern California
Fast growing to 60–70 feet tall and one third as wide; pyramidal with wide-spreading, pendulous branches

The branches of this graceful tree end in lacy sprays of bright green to blue-green. Other distinguishing features are its nodding tip and soft brown to reddish brown fibrous bark.

Many cultivars are available, varying in form and foliage color. This tree is subject to cypress root rot in the Northwest. Check with a county extension agent for rot-resistant varieties.

Chamaecyparis nootkatensis
Alaska cedar

Needled evergreen
Zones 5–9
Native to Alaska, British Columbia, and northern Oregon
Moderate growing to 70–100 feet; narrow, columnar habit with strong, irregular branching and pendulous branch tips

The dark green foliage of this tree has a characteristic and strong fragrance when crushed. Alaska cedar needs full sun and thrives in moist, well-drained, acid soil. It is native to harsh climates and tolerates low temperatures. This is a beautiful and durable landscape tree.

Chamaecyparis obtusa
Hinoki false-cypress

Needled evergreen
Zones 5–8
Native to Japan
Moderate growing to 40–50 feet tall and 15–25 feet wide; pyramidal

The foliage of this tree is a deep, shiny green in thick, horizontally flattened sprays. Branch tips are slightly pendulous.

Many varieties, including many well-known dwarf forms, are available. Some of the favorites follow.

'Crippsii' has golden new growth and reaches a mature height of 30 feet.

'Gracilis', with its very dark, shiny green foliage and somewhat weeping form, grows to 20 feet high by 4 to 5 feet wide at maturity.

'Nana Gracilis' is a very compact variety and may grow to less than 10 feet.

Chamaecyparis pisifera
Sawara false-cypress

Needled evergreen
Zones 4–8
Native to Japan
Moderate growing to 20–40 feet tall and half as wide; pyramidal

This tree is less dense than *C. obtusa*. The loosely arranged, scalelike leaves of the species

are bright, glossy green. Lower branches are sometimes lost early in life, revealing reddish brown bark that peels in long strips. Inner branches often die out; encourage new growth with annual pruning.

Chionanthus virginicus
Fringe tree

Deciduous
Zones 4–9
Native to the southeastern United States
Slow growing to 20–30 feet with a round crown; wider than tall

The foliage of the fringe tree is heavy textured and bold, very similar to that of a magnolia. It turns yellow in autumn. Foliage and flowers show late in the spring, well after danger of frost has passed.

The flowers have white, threadlike petals that form fleecy clusters. These delicate blooms are aromatic and persist into early summer. Clusters of dark blue berries follow the flowers on female trees and are a favorite of many birds.

Chionanthus virginicus
(fringe tree)

Cornus florida (flowering dogwood)

This is a good tree for a small space. It works especially well near a patio. Deep rooted and multitrunked (almost more of a shrub than a tree), it requires special shaping or training if a tree form is desired.

Cinnamomum camphora
Camphor tree

Evergreen
Zones 9, 10
Native to China and Japan
Slow growing to 50 feet tall or higher with wider spread; round headed, with limbs spreading upward

The camphor tree creates dense shade and is a popular residential and street tree in the southern United States. Attractive, aromatic, shiny, yellow-green foliage contrasts with the reddish new leaves. Yellow flower clusters are fragrant although not showy. The camphor tree makes a good street tree if given sufficient space in which to grow. It does poorly in heavy, alkaline soils.

Cladrastis lutea
Yellowwood

Deciduous
Zones 4–9
Native from North Carolina to Kentucky
Slow growing to 30–35 feet tall and 20–25 feet wide; upright, with spreading branches forming a vase-shaped crown

Yellowwood has attractive, smooth, beechlike gray bark and clean foliage that turns clear yellow in the fall. Its most notable feature, however, is its show of pure white, intensely fragrant flowers, pea shaped and borne in clusters like white wisteria. Flowering occurs in May or June and is heavier in alternate years.

Brown pods and bare, zigzagging branches provide winter interest. This is a good lawn, patio, or park tree, although it is slow growing and won't bloom until it's ten years old. When mature, yellowwood withstands drought, heat, and extreme cold and tolerates alkaline and wet soils. It is a good tree for urban sites.

CORNUS
DOGWOOD

The dogwoods include plants that range in size from the 6- to 9-inch bunchberry of the northern woodlands to the Pacific dogwoods, which may grow 70 feet or more in height. In general, dogwoods require a slightly acidic soil with moderate moisture and good fertility. They will grow well in full sun except in hot climates, where they must be partially shaded. Dogwoods are well known for their beautiful foliage and flowers.

Cornus alternifolia
Pagoda dogwood

Deciduous
Zones 5–9
Native to North America, Europe, and Asia
Grows to 15–25 feet tall and equally wide

Pagoda dogwood is less showy than other species, but it is hardier and is useful in harsh climates. Its branches are arranged in distinct, horizontal tiers, which make an appealing winter silhouette. This species

has light green leaves that turn red in the fall.

Cornus florida
Flowering dogwood

Deciduous
Zones 5–9
Native to the eastern United States
Moderate growing, rarely exceeding 30 feet; variable habit from pyramidal to umbrella to wide spreading and flat

The flowering dogwood is an attractive and interesting tree the year around. The display of flowers in the spring is wonderfully showy. In the fall, the leaves turn a rich red and crimson. The glossy, red berries are borne in clusters and often persist after the leaves have fallen. In winter, the layered branching habit and the myriad conspicuous flower buds are decorative. This tree grows best in rich, moist, acidic soil and in light shade. If stressed, flowering dogwood is susceptible to fungal disease and to borer problems.

Cornus kousa (kousa dogwood, Japanese dogwood)

Cotinus coggygria (smoke tree)

A number of varieties of this species are available. Among these are the following.

'Cherokee Chief' is a pink flowering dogwood. It has a deep, rich color, but it is not as winter hardy as other pink dogwoods.

'Cloud Nine', a profuse white bloomer, is noted for the many large flowers borne on even a young tree. It is slow growing and smaller than most of the other varieties, and so is a good choice for planting where space is limited. It does not do well in areas with cold winters.

'New Hampshire', one of the hardiest of all the selections of *Cornus florida,* blooms regularly each year in southern Vermont and New Hampshire, where it originated. It cannot tolerate hot southern summers.

Cornus florida var. *rubra* is the naturally occurring pink form of flowering dogwood. Its pink color varies somewhat, depending on the soil in which it is grown, the age of the flowers, and its genetic background.

Cornus kousa
Kousa dogwood,
Japanese dogwood

Deciduous
Zones 5–9
Native to Japan, China, and Korea
Moderate growing to 15–30 feet, spreading; tends to be multitrunked

This species blooms later than other flowering dogwoods. It turns yellow and scarlet in the fall and bears red fruit that is favored by birds. It can be either grown as a multi-stemmed large shrub or trained as a single-stemmed small tree. It has a delicate limb structure and shiny, green, 4-inch-long leaves. Several cultivars selected for increased vigor and hardiness are available.

Cotinus coggygria
Smoke tree

Deciduous
Zones 5–9
Native to southern Europe and central China
Moderate growing to 15–25 feet tall and equally wide; broad, urn-shaped with rounded top

This is actually a shrub, but a little pruning can produce an attractive, multitrunked tree form. This species blooms at the beginning of summer and as the flowers fade, they become feathery masses of fine gray or purplish hairs that give the tree a smokelike appearance. This lasts throughout the summer. Leaf color is blue-green in summer, yellow to orange-red in the fall.

The smoke tree prefers good drainage and blooms best in infertile, dry soils. It is drought tolerant and easy to grow.

CRATAEGUS
HAWTHORN

The hawthorns are a group of thorny, small trees that are among the most rugged of the flowering trees. Most species bear white flowers, have showy red or orange fruits, and thrive even in the city, along highways, and at the seashore where salt spray is a hazard to most trees. They are, however, susceptible to fire blight. Hawthorns bloom in late May. Many species have fine, glossy foliage, and the fruit of most is very long lasting.

Crataegus laevigata (C. oxyacantha)
English hawthorn

Deciduous
Zones 5–7
Native to England and Europe
Moderate growing to 15–25 feet high and equally wide; round headed, low branching

Although common, this species does not do as well as other hawthorns when grown in the United States. Summer heat and humidity tax it severely: The leaves, being subject to fungus-related diseases, drop off to leave the twigs bare during most of the summer. Several cultivars offer some resistance to fungus damage and leaf drop.

'Alba Plena' bears a myriad of double, pure white flowers in late May that gradually turn pale pink. It has very little fruit but holds its foliage quite well in the East.

Crataegus laevigata (English hawthorn)

Crataegus phaenopyrum (Washington thorn)

'Crimson Cloud' bears lots of bright, crimson flowers, each with a white star in the center. The foliage is leathery, fine textured, and resistant to leaf spot disease. The fruit is glossy red. This cultivar grows into a tall, oval tree 20 feet in height. It tolerates city conditions.

Crataegus × *lavallei*
Lavalle hawthorn

Deciduous
Zones 5–9
Hybrid of *C. crus-galli* and
C. pubescens
Moderate growing to 20 feet with a dense, oval head

The white flowers of the lavalle hawthorn are large and abundant, and the foliage is glossy green in summer and bronze red in the fall. This species bears orange to red fruits that remain on the tree well into the winter.

Crataegus monogyna 'Stricta'
Singleseed hawthorn

Deciduous
Zones 5–9

Native to England and Europe
Grows to 20–30 feet tall and 8–9 feet wide with upright branches and a narrow habit

The singleseed hawthorn is often used as an understock for the grafted varieties of hawthorn and, in England, as a hedge plant. This variety is one of the best narrow trees for urban situations. It is almost completely thornless and bears white flowers in small clusters in late May.

Crataegus phaenopyrum
Washington thorn

Deciduous
Zones 5–9
Native to the southern United States
Grows to 20–30 feet tall and 20–25 feet wide; broad, columnar, and dense with thorns

The Washington thorn has glossy foliage that turns a beautiful orange-red in the fall. It is considered the best of all the hawthorns for fall color. Flowers are abundant and pure white, giving rise to large clusters of scarlet fruit that is

among the longest lasting of all the species. This tree is quite narrow and upright when young; it broadens with age. Washington thorn is resistant to fire blight and grows well in the city.

Crataegus punctata
Dotted hawthorn

Deciduous
Zones 5–9
Native to the United States and Canada
Grows to 30 feet

This is a hardy, drought-tolerant native species with attractive silvery bark and abundant fruit. It is one of the few species that will bear yellow as well as red fruit. The cultivar 'Ohio Pioneer' is valued because it is virtually thornless and therefore useful for garden or street planting.

Crataegus 'Toba'

Deciduous
Zones 4–9
Hybrid of *C. succulenta* and
C. laevigata 'Paulii'
Grows to 15–20 feet

This hardy hawthorn originated in the harsh climate of Manitoba, Canada. Its flowers are borne abundantly every year and are pure white when they first open, gradually deepening to a rose color. The tree fruits rather sparsely, and the leathery foliage is a fine, dark green color. This variety is resistant to leaf spot disease and is almost thornless. It is a useful flowering garden tree, especially in cold areas.

Crataegus viridis 'Winter King'
Winter King hawthorn

Deciduous
Zones 5–9
Native to the southern United States
Grows to 35 feet with a rounded, dense head

This tree has distinct silvery gray stems with a waxy bloom and fine, glossy leaves. It produces abundant and long-lasting red fruit and has attractive, exfoliating, silver-colored bark. It has vase-shaped branches when young, forming a full, rounded head when mature.

Cryptomeria japonica
(Japanese cedar)

× *Cupressocyparis leylandii* (Leyland cypress)

Cupressus macrocarpa
(Monterey cypress)

Cryptomeria japonica
Japanese cedar

Needled evergreen
Zones 5-9
Native to Japan and China
Moderate growing to 60-90
feet tall and half as wide;
pyramidal, open form; rounded
top with age

Its small, green needles and
drooping branches give this
tree a soft, graceful look. The
needles pick up a bronze tinge
in winter; the reddish brown
bark peels in strips.

This tree needs room to develop and is a good park tree. It
likes ample water (it does not
do well in arid climates) and
well-drained, deep soil. This
species is relatively pest free.

'Elegans', the plume cedar,
has soft, feathery foliage that
turns coppery bronze in winter.
It is slow growing to a
20- to 25-foot dense pyramid.
Many cultivars, including
dwarf forms, are available.

'Lobbii' is a dense, compact
tree and a fine conifer for
streets and large landscapes
and parks. It is more heat
resistant and holds its form
better than other varieties.
'Lobbii' has short, dense tufts
of needles that remain green
through the winter, and the
crown is conical even in older
trees. Many larger *Cryptomeria japonica* in the United
States are of this clone.

× Cupressocyparis leylandii
Leyland cypress

Needled evergreen
Zones 6-10
Hybrid of *Cupressus
macrocarpa* and
Chamaecyparis nootkatensis
Fast growing to 40-50 feet;
columnar, loosely pyramidal
with age

This is one of the best fast-
growing columnar plants for
tall hedges and screens. Re-
ports of its growth rate range
from 3 to 5 feet per year. The
branching pattern is graceful,
spreading in horizontal fans of
gray-green to pale green foliage. This tree is dense when
young. It tolerates a wide range
of soils and climates, and many
cultivars are available.

CUPRESSUS
CYPRESS

These trees vary widely in
form and shape—some are
windswept, others dramatically
tall and narrow. Most are
grown on the West Coast, although a few are seen in the
southeast. All are large, fragrant evergreens with scalelike
leaves and small cones.
Cypresses are excellent specimen or accent trees in the
right setting and climate. They
thrive in mild, dry weather and
full sun.

Cupressus glabra
Smooth Arizona cypress

Needled evergreen
Zones 7-10
Native to central Arizona
Fast growing to 35 feet tall and
half as wide; compact, narrow,
pyramidal, becoming more
open with age

This cypress can withstand
hot, dry, desert conditions and
poor, sandy soil. Its straight
trunk has reddish bark that
eventually becomes brown and
furrowed with age. The scalelike foliage is silver gray to
blue-green. Smooth Arizona cypress is a good windbreak,
screen, or hedge. Wet soil en-
courages shallow roots, which
weakens the wind resistance.

Cupressus macrocarpa
Monterey cypress

Needled evergreen
Zones 8-10
Native to the Monterey
peninsula in California
Slow to moderate growing to
40-70 feet; narrow, pyramidal,
becoming rounded with age

This tree is often associated
with the California coastline.
Its characteristic windswept
habit develops properly only in
high winds near the coast, and
even then only with age. Young
trees are symmetrical. This
tree should not be grown far
from the West Coast. It is valuable as a windbreak or clipped
hedge, but is subject to fatal
canker disease. Ask a county
extension agent for information about the prevention and
control of this disease.

Diospyros kaki (kaki persimmon, Japanese persimmon)

Eriobotrya japonica (loquat)

Cupressus sempervirens
(Italian cypress)

Cupressus sempervirens
Italian cypress

Evergreen
Zones 8–10
Native to southern Europe and western Asia
Fast growing to 30–40 feet tall and 3–6 feet wide in a strict vertical column

Italian cypress can be a dominant vertical element in any landscape but is best suited to a large garden due to its vertical habit, mature size, and formal aspect.

This cypress tolerates a wide range of soils and drought, but not poor drainage. Its scalelike, dark green leaves are borne on horizontal branches.

Several cultivars are more widely available than the species. Most have tight habits and vary in foliage color from bright green to blue.

DIOSPYROS
PERSIMMON

Persimmons give excellent summer shade and bear attractive and edible fruit.

Some species are hardy to -20° F. With pruning persimmons can be used in a small yard and are outstanding alone or against a background of evergreens. They should be planted in full sun and in places where falling fruit will not be a problem.

The fruit of the the American and some Japanese varieties is very astringent until fully ripe. Grafted trees can bear in two years. Persimmon leaves will fall, leaving the bright orange fruit to decorate the tree. The fruit can be eaten fresh or can be frozen, dried, or left to freeze on the tree and eaten like popsicles.

Diospyros kaki
Kaki persimmon,
Japanese persimmon

Deciduous
Zones 7–9
Native to China and Korea
Moderate growing to 20–30 feet with a similar spread; low, round head

Kaki persimmon foliage, when new, is a soft, light green. It gradually turns a heavier dark green in the summer and different shades of yellow, red, and orange in the fall. Falling leaves expose bright orange, sweet fruit. The visible bark is also attractive.

This is a fine shade tree for a small garden. Stretch its hardiness by planting it in portable containers or as an espalier against a south wall. Few pests bother this tree. Constant moisture and early spring fertilizing will help reduce fruit drop.

Choice fruiting varieties include 'Chocolate', 'Fuyu', and 'Hachiya', the latter being also the most valuable as an ornamental tree.

Diospyros virginiana
American common persimmon

Deciduous
Zones 5–9
Native to the eastern
United States
Moderate growing to 30–50 feet tall and half as wide;
oval form

The American persimmon is hardier than other persimmon species. It is easily identified by what appear to be small boxes deeply cut into the bark. The fruit of this tree ripens after the first frost, turning from sour to sweet. This tree does not have the striking show of fruit on bare branches, but it does provide an interesting winter branch silhouette.

More widely adapted than the Japanese persimmon, the American persimmon tolerates a broad range of soils and climates. Male and female trees are required for fruit production. Especially good-tasting cultivars are available from specialty growers.

Eriobotrya japonica
Loquat

Evergreen
Zones 7–9
Native to China and Japan
Moderate growing to 30 feet high and equally wide; broad, round, crownless

This is an ornamental tree with edible fruit. Its most striking feature is its very large leaves, 6 to 12 inches long by 2 to 4 inches wide, prominently veined and serrated, dark green above with downy, rust-

Erythrina humeana (Natal coral tree)

Eucalyptus ficifolia (flaming gum, red-flowering gum)

colored undersides. The fragrant but small white flowers appear in the fall and are followed by abundant orange to yellow fruit that ripens in late winter or early spring.

This tree is amenable to pruning and can even be trained as a ground cover. It is also used as a landscape specimen, espalier, or in a container.

Loquats tolerate alkaline soil but need good drainage and are sometimes subject to fire blight.

The seedlings have unpredictable fruit quality, but the cultivars are reliable. 'Gold Nugget' and 'Champagne' produce good-tasting fruit.

Erythrina humeana
Natal coral tree

Deciduous
Zone 10
Native to South Africa
Fast growing to 25 feet; spreading; most useful when multitrunked

The bright orange-red flowers of the Natal coral tree are held well above the dark green foliage. Blooms appear primarily during fall, but in a warm,

sheltered location the bloom period may be longer. This is a good garden-sized tree that blooms even in its early years.

EUCALYPTUS
EUCALYPTUS, GUM

There are nearly 600 species of eucalyptus, all evergreen and native to Australia. Many have proved adaptable to the climate and landscape of California. Eucalyptus are fast growing and essentially maintenance free. Their litter of leaves and seedpods can be a problem, however, and some consider eucalyptus trees unwanted invaders.

Because of their exceedingly rapid growth, eucalyptus trees should be set out at the smallest practicable size and left unstaked.

Eucalyptus camaldulensis
Murray River red gum

Evergreen
Zones 9, 10
Native to Australia
Rapid growing to 75 feet with

upright, spreading crown and pendant foliage of long, narrow leaves

This species is considered one of the best of the big eucalyptus if there is plenty of planting space. It has an attractive, mottled trunk that often sheds rough, corky bark at its base. Stringy bark may peel from the branches intermittently. In some cases, the slender branches hang straight down for 10 to 15 feet. When established, this species manages well under a range of conditions from desert heat to heavy rainfall.

Eucalyptus cinerea
Florist's eucalyptus

Evergreen
Zones 9, 10
Native to Australia
Moderate to rapid growing to 30–40 feet

The florist's eucalyptus has perfoliate (naturally united around the stem) leaves in its juvenile stage that are often used by florists either alone or with cut flowers. A good percentage of these young

leaves are retained as the long, narrow, mature leaves develop. The rough brown bark has a distinctive ashen tone that inspired the species name, *cinerea* (ash colored). This species tends to have multiple trunks but can be pruned to one. It remains garden sized for at least the first 10 years and is considered a striking specimen for the first 5.

Eucalyptus ficifolia
Flaming gum,
red-flowering gum

Evergreen
Zone 10
Native to Australia
Rapid growing to 25 feet

This tree does well in frost-free coastal conditions and is attractive when in full bloom. Its flowers come in a variety of colors but are often a bright red. Its leaves are dark green, large, and heavy, and resemble those of the ficus, hence its name *ficifolia* (like a ficus). This gum has a chunky form, with foliage so thick the branches are virtually hidden.

Eucalyptus polyanthemos (silver-dollar eucalyptus)

Fagus sylvatica (European beech)

Eucalyptus globulus
Blue gum

Evergreen
Zones 9, 10
Native to Australia
Fast growing to 150–200 feet;
tall, straight form

This tree has sickle-shaped, dark green leaves, 6 to 10 inches long. Its flowers are a creamy white or yellow and appear in winter and spring. These are followed by rough, bumpy, blue-gray seed capsules. Constant shedding bark, leaf drop, and fruit fall make this a messy tree. The wood is brittle, and branches break easily in high winds. This species has been widely planted as a forest tree in California but is not appropriate for gardens or yards.

Eucalyptus polyanthemos
Silver-dollar eucalyptus

Evergreen
Zones 9, 10
Native to Australia
Fast growing to 40–50 feet

The silvery gray juvenile leaves of this species are rounded and suspended individually on light twigs. This is a good, tough tree, and it grows quite rapidly. It does well on the seacoast or in the desert, but it dislikes wet places. This is an attractive tree when young but may be less appealing with age.

Fagus sylvatica
European beech

Deciduous
Zones 5–7
Native to central and southern Europe
Slow growing to 70–80 feet tall and 60 feet wide; dense, pyramidal form

European beech is valued for its smooth, gray bark and glossy, dark green foliage, which takes on a yellow-bronze color in the fall. The edible nuts attract wildlife.

Beeches need lots of room to grow properly. They are often found in groves, where their silvery gray bark brings a brightness to the area, even on cloudy days. The lower branches of the beech should be allowed to sweep the ground, which means it may require an area of 50 to 60 feet in diameter to fully expand. This characteristic makes it most suitable for parks, golf courses, college campuses, and very large gardens.

'Asplenifolia', fernleaf beech, has refined, fernlike foliage, as the common name suggests.

'Pendula', weeping European beech, is considered one of the best weeping trees. Its dark green foliage grows on graceful, pendant branches that sweep the ground.

'Riversii', River's purple beech, is considered by some to be the most beautiful of all purple-foliage trees. It resists drought but grows best in moist soil conditions.

FRAXINUS
ASH

This is a large and versatile group of trees, generally able to take wet soils with poor drainage. The ash is particularly valued for its leaves. With a few exceptions, they are 6 to 12 inches long and divided into as many as 12 to 13 leaflets that can each be

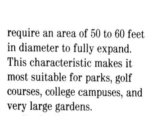

several inches long. The leaves combine to form a beautiful, softly textured canopy casting a shade light enough to allow grass and other plants to grow beneath.

Some consider the heavy seed production and resulting seedlings a drawback of the ash. A variety of seedless cultivars are now available, however, making this less of a complaint.

Fraxinus americana
White ash

Deciduous
Zones 3–9
Native to the eastern United States
Fast growing to 80–100 feet, spreading to not quite half as wide with a rounded top

The dense, compound leaves of the white ash have seven to nine leaflets, each 4 to 6 inches long. They are a light gray-green in summer and turn pale yellow to orange to purple in the fall. Male and female flowers are inconspicuous and on separate trees. The white ash's papery seedpod is 2 inches long, and its gray bark has a

Fraxinus ornus (flowering ash)

Fraxinus pennsylvanica (F. lanceolata) (green ash, red ash)

long, narrow diamond pattern, especially on older trees. This is a good shade tree or windbreak and may do well where other trees have done poorly.

Seed litter and insufficient growing space are this tree's drawbacks. Some cultivars eliminate these concerns. 'Autumn Purple' is a seedless selection with good autumn tints. 'Rosehill' is also seedless and grows to 50 feet or less. Its adaptation is limited to zones 5 to 9.

Fraxinus ornus

Flowering ash

Deciduous
Zones 6-8
Native to southern Europe and western Asia
Fast growing to 35 feet with a round head

The flowering ash does best in cooler areas. It bears fluffy white to greenish white clusters of fragrant flowers in late spring, and its shiny green leaves turn soft lavender or yellow in fall. The seed clusters are unattractive and remain on the tree well into winter.

Fraxinus pennsylvanica (F. lanceolata)

Green ash, red ash

Deciduous
Zones 3-8
Native to Nova Scotia and to Georgia and Mississippi
Fast growing to 30-50 feet; narrowly upright when young; later forms a compact, rounded crown

This is a popular ash and is considered easy to grow. It will withstand wet soil and severe cold and is also drought resistant. 'Marshall's Seedless', as its name indicates, is a seedless and therefore litter-free cultivar.

Ginkgo biloba

Maidenhair tree

Deciduous
Zones 4-9
Native to China
Slow growing to 60-100 feet, although growth rate varies with climate; conical and sparsely branched in youth, spreading and dense with age

The maidenhair tree has a picturesque, irregular habit of growth and bright green, fan-shaped leaves. The leaves turn brilliant yellow in fall and often drop all at once—sometimes overnight.

This remarkably tough tree will tolerate smoke and air pollution and ranks as one of the top street trees. It is pest free and widely adaptable, demanding only a well-drained soil. It needs room to develop and is excellent as a park or large lawn tree. It will need extra water after transplanting but is otherwise relatively trouble free.

The seeds of the female maidenhair tree are highly valued in China and Japan, where they are roasted and eaten. In the United States the seeds are considered a nuisance, and typically only male clones are purchased and planted.

Gleditsia triacanthos var. inermis

Thornless common honeylocust

Deciduous
Zones 5-9
Native to the eastern and central United States

Moderate to fast growing to 30-80 feet tall and equally wide

The delicate, compound leaf of the honeylocust has tiny leaflets that allow filtered sunlight to pass through. The lacy appearance gives the tree a tropical look, rare among trees hardy enough to live in the northern United States.

The honeylocust facilitates lawn development by leafing out late in the spring and dropping its golden leaflets early in the fall. This allows turf to grow vigorously during its preferred seasons—early spring and late fall—when the weather is cool and moist. This, in addition to its light shade, make the common honeylocust a particularly good lawn tree. Moreover, the leaflets require a minimum of raking.

Honeylocust is quite tolerant of various environmental stresses, including air pollution and highway salting. It is also somewhat resistant to heavy winds. The upright branching habit, especially of young trees, allows them to survive much ice storm damage as well.

Ginkgo biloba (maidenhair tree)

Gleditsia triacanthos var. *inermis* (thornless common honeylocust)

Halesia carolina (Carolina silver bell)

In spite of its advantages, the honeylocust does have some problems, especially in warmer climates. Mimosa webworm can be troublesome in some areas. Check locally to determine if this or other pests are prevalent. Wilt is also a problem in some places along the East Coast.

The following are some of the many cultivars that have been developed.

'Imperial' has a moderate growth rate to 35 feet. The round crown is symmetrical and spreading. The bright green foliage casts heavy shade because of the closely spaced leaves and dense branching.

'Majestic' is compact with a fast growth rate to 45 to 55 feet. This tree is not as dense as 'Skyline' or 'Imperial'. It has a spreading crown and dark green foliage.

'Moraine' is fast growing to 40 to 50 feet and is vase shaped. The trunk is sometimes curved when young and may require training if a straight trunk is desired.

'Ruby Lace', with its fast-growing, spreading habit,

reaches 30 to 35 feet. The new foliage is purplish bronze, maturing to green. This cultivar may need extra pruning in youth.

'Shademaster' is a fast grower to 40 to 50 feet. The upright, spreading branches form a wineglass shape. Its dark green foliage lasts longer than that of other selections.

'Skyline' is also a fast grower, usually reaching 40 to 45 feet. It has a pyramidal form. The leaves are dark green, compact, leathery, and larger than others.

'Sunburst' grows quickly to 30 to 35 feet with an upright, spreading habit. The new foliage is yellow, gradually turning green.

Gymnocladus dioica
Kentucky coffee tree

Deciduous
Zones 4–8
Native to North America
Moderate growing to 60–90 feet tall, half as wide; open, upright-oval shape

This tree is valued for its feathery leaves that are 1½ to

3 feet long and divided into numerous leaflets 1 inch to 3 inches long. It is also an attractive winter tree, with its picturesque branches and stubby twigs. This is a good accent tree where space allows. Fragrant flowers are born in inconspicuous green-white panicles. Nonfruiting male trees are good as street trees. The fruit (borne on female trees) is long, wide, brown pods that create a nuisance when they fall to the ground.

This tree likes sun or partial shade and fertile soil, but tolerates dry soil and city pollution. It gets its common name from the fact that its seeds were used as a coffee substitute during the Civil War.

Halesia carolina
Carolina silver bell

Deciduous
Zones 5–9
Native to the southeastern United States
Slow to moderate growing to 25–30 feet; pyramidal in youth, round headed with age

This is considered one of the most attractive American natives. It is popular in England and in Europe and is becoming more widely planted on the East Coast of the United States, its country of origin. In mid-May, each branch bears a string of 1-inch-long white flowers that resemble little bells hanging down on slender stems. This tree grows naturally in a clump formation with several stems but can be pruned to one when young. It makes a fine shelter plant when combined with an underplanting of azaleas or rhododendrons.

ILEX
HOLLY

There are 300 or so different species of holly. They range from dwarf shrubs to 70-foot trees and grow in the temperate and tropical regions of both hemispheres.

Some hollies have spiny leaves; others have leaves with smooth margins. The fruit is black, red, yellow, or orange, depending upon the species or

Ilex aquifolium (English holly)

Jacaranda acutifolia (jacaranda)

variety. Usually, both male and female plants are needed for the female to produce berries. One male plant will normally pollinate most female plants within 900 feet.

In general, hollies do best in acidic soil and in full sunlight. They tolerate partial shade but become leggy in dense shade.

English and American hollies are attacked by two kinds of leafminers, usually from April to mid-May. The most common one makes blotches on the leaves, the other a serpentine pattern. Scale and spider mites may also be a problem.

Ilex aquifolium
English holly

Evergreen
Zones 7–9
Native to Europe and northern Africa
Moderate growing to 50 feet tall and 20 feet wide

This is the holly many associate with Christmas. It often has spiny, glossy, dark green leaves, but many silver and golden variegated forms are available. Smooth-leaved

forms can also be found. Berry color varies from red to cream. This species is best grown in the Pacific Northwest where summers are cool and winters are mild.

The following are some of the better-known cultivars.

'Angustifolia' has a narrow, conical form with small, narrow leaves. Usually the male form is available.

'Boulder Creek' is a California selection with very large, dark green, glossy leaves and a heavy, upright growth. Its berries are a brilliant red.

'Little Bull' has smaller leaves and is more compact than others of this species. It is a good pollinator and highly ornamental.

Ilex opaca
American holly

Evergreen
Zones 5–9
Native to the eastern United States
Grows to 45–50 feet; pyramidal

Through the use of hardy cultivars, this holly has been successfully grown north of its original home. Hardy cultivars

have withstood temperatures lower than -24° F. However, when this tree is planted in more northerly regions it becomes more selective in its site requirements. In the southeast, American holly will grow on moist or wet sites. In the north, it requires good drainage and protection from severe winds.

American holly foliage is evergreen, and the leaves are usually spiny. The color of the berries varies from red to orange to yellow, but red is most common.

More than a thousand selections of American holly have been named. Hardy red-berried forms include 'Angelica', 'Arlene Leach', 'Betty Pride', 'Carnival', 'Cumberland', 'Mary Holman', 'Red Flush', and 'Valentine'. 'Canary' or 'Morgan Gold' offer yellow berries. 'Jersey Knight' and 'Santa Claus' are two male cultivars.

'Kentucky Smoothleaf' is a nonspiny variety that is somewhat tender and should be planted in protected locations or restricted to the southern states. 'East Palatka' is also a southern smooth-leaved holly.

'Savannah' is another southern selection, prized for its heavy set of red berries. 'Jersey Princess' has especially rich, dark, glossy green foliage.

Jacaranda acutifolia
Jacaranda

Deciduous
Zone 10
Native to Brazil
Moderate to fast growing to 25–50 feet tall and two thirds as wide; open, irregular head, often multitrunked

One of the most attractive warm-climate trees, the jacaranda flowers over a long period, usually from May to July. It is deciduous for only a short time, and its seedpods are often used in dried displays.

This tree is tolerant of a variety of conditions but becomes floppy with too much water, dwarfed with too little. It needs good drainage and is not likely to do well in areas with high coastal winds. Extra training is necessary to develop its best form. The jacaranda is a good choice for the garden or along the street.

Juglans nigra (black walnut)

Juniperus virginiana (eastern red cedar)

Koelreuteria paniculata (goldenrain tree)

JUGLANS
WALNUT

Almost 20 different species of these large, spreading trees are found in the temperate and tropical regions of the world. Many of these species provide lumber, edible nuts, and shade. In the United States the two species most commonly seen are black walnut and Persian or English walnut.

Juglans nigra
Black walnut

Deciduous
Zones 4–8
Native to the eastern United States and southeastern Canada
Fast growing to 100–150 feet

This large tree, with its straight trunk and open, rounded crown, is popular as a shade tree in large yards. The bark is thick and furrowed and becomes nearly black with age. The yellow-green leaves are 8 to 25 inches long and consist of 15 to 23 leaflets. The 1½- to 2½-inch-long edible nuts are sweet and oily. The black walnut is toxic to neighboring plants, however, and is often defoliated by leaf spot disease by August.

Juglans regia
Persian walnut,
English walnut

Deciduous
Zones 6–10
Native from southeastern Europe to China
Fast growing to 60–100 feet

The Persian or English walnut tree is highly desirable for its edible nut crop. These are the prepared walnuts most often found commercially. This species is not desirable as a shade tree, in spite of its large canopy. The fruit is messy, and the honeydew from aphid infestations will stain patios, walkways, or cars beneath the tree.

JUNIPERUS
JUNIPER

This is a very large group of plants that range in size from low-spreading ground covers to tall, columnar trees. Species available vary by climate. A wide variety of selections is available within each species.

Two similar forms with different adaptations are discussed here. Each is usually sold only by its various cultivars and is selected for foliage color and a columnar growth habit.

Juniperus scopulorum
Rocky Mountain juniper

Needled evergreen
Zones 4–7
Native to the Rocky Mountains
Slow growing to 35–45 feet; broad, pyramidal form becomes round topped with age

This is the best juniper for areas of heat and drought. It does poorly in places with high summer rainfall or humidity. Its foliage is blue-gray and its bark brownish red. This juniper makes an excellent tall hedge, screen, or windbreak. Many selections, varying in foliage color and form, are available.

Juniperus virginiana
Eastern red cedar

Needled evergreen
Zones 3–7

Native to the eastern United States
Slow growing to 35–45 feet; pyramidal

The eastern red cedar is adaptable to a wide range of soils and climates. It will take summer rain as well as drought. Normally it has bright green foliage, but several selected varieties vary both in foliage color and form. This tree turns pinkish in cold winter weather. Its attractive blue berries are a favorite winter bird food. This species makes an excellent and long-lived tall hedge, screen, or windbreak. Many cultivars are available.

Koelreuteria paniculata
Goldenrain tree

Deciduous
Zones 5–9
Native to China, Japan, and Korea
Moderate growing to 25–35 feet; rounded outline, wide-spreading, open branches eventually developing to a flat top

The goldenrain tree tolerates wind, alkaline soil, salt spray,

Laburnum × *watereri* 'Vossii' (goldenchain tree)

Lagerstroemia indica (crape myrtle)

fall and winter low temperatures, and, once established, long periods without much water. It is a well-behaved tree, although the branches may be brittle. The deep root system and the open branching habit make this a good lawn tree.

Starting in April, new foliage develops quickly, filling the tree with soft, medium-green, divided leaves. By late spring or summer the flower spikes begin to open and the tree is completely covered with a mass of yellow flowers, often visited by honeybees. If the tree is kept watered, the flowers begin to set small fruits, which develop an outer husk and look like Chinese lanterns. Later in the summer, the fruits mature to a dark copper tan and hang in clusters late into the fall.

Laburnum × watereri 'Vossii'

Goldenchain tree

Deciduous
Zones 5–7
Hybrid of *L. alpinum* and
L. anagyroides

Moderate growing to 20–30 feet; dense, upright, vase-shaped crown

This tree is most often planted for its flowers. In May it bears 18-inch, tapering clusters of rich yellow, pea-shaped flowers that resemble wisteria blooms. This is not an attractive tree when out of bloom. Its leaves, fruit, and flowers are all very poisonous, and it does not do well in hot climates.

LAGERSTROEMIA
CRAPE MYRTLE

These deciduous, flowering small trees or neat shrubs are vase shaped and easy to grow in the right conditions. They resemble lilacs in flower shape, and some are vaguely similar in fragrance. Their bloom continues for weeks and weeks. Some new varieties are hardy as far north as Washington, D.C. At the northern edge of their range or in very hard winters, they may die back to the ground but grow back from the roots and bloom

again on new wood. In colder climates they can be grown in containers and taken into a garage over the winter. They are excellent as accents and will bloom when very small. Flower color ranges from pink to red or white, and some species have good fall color. All have interesting, mottled bark. These trees need sun to flower, do best in slightly acid loam, and will tolerate drought once established.

Lagerstroemia fauriei

Japanese crape myrtle

Deciduous
Zones 6–9
Native to Japan
Slow growing to 12–14 feet; vase shaped

This myrtle is very similar to *L. indica,* but with smaller white blossoms and no fall color. The bark is especially attractive, peeling brown and red.

The outstanding feature of this species is its resistance to powdery mildew, which makes it easier to grow than other species in moist coastal areas.

Lagerstroemia indica
Crape myrtle

Deciduous
Zones 7–10
Native to China
Slow growing to 10–30 feet; vase shaped as a multitrunked tree, round headed when trained to a single stem

Crape myrtle is best known for its late-summer profusion of showy pink, red, lavender, or white flowers. The flowers are crinkled and ruffled like crepe paper and held high above the foliage. The bark is peeling red and brown, attractive the year around, and striking in winter. The fall color is good but somewhat inconsistent.

This myrtle will mildew in moist coastal locations and so should be planted in areas with good air circulation.

Several cultivars of greater hardiness, mildew resistance, and vigor, collectively called Indian Tribe crape myrtles, have been introduced. Notable among these is 'Catawba', with its good orange-red fall color and dark purple blossoms.

Laurus nobilis (sweet bay, bay laurel, Grecian laurel)

Leucodendron argenteum (silver tree)

Liquidambar styraciflua (American sweet gum)

Larix kaempferi (L. leptolepis)
Japanese larch

Deciduous
Zones 5–8
Native to Japan
Fast growing to 50–60 feet tall and 25–40 feet wide; spreading, pyramidal form

That it is deciduous and has good fall color sets this feathery conifer apart. It is broader and hardier than the European larch and its foliage is blue-green in summer, brilliant yellow-orange in fall.

Laurus nobilis
Sweet bay, bay laurel, Grecian laurel

Evergreen
Zones 8–10
Native to Greece
Slow growing to 12–30 feet; compact, conical form

This is a well-behaved, indoor-outdoor tree. It has a sophisticated look and can be sheared into hedges, screens, or formal shapes. The leaves are aromatic and dark green and are widely used in cooking as bay seasoning. The inconspicuous

flowers are followed by small, dark berries, which attract birds. This tree requires well-drained soil. It will tolerate city conditions and works well as a wall tree.

Leucodendron argenteum
Silver tree

Evergreen
Zone 10
Native to South Africa
Grows to 30–35 feet

The silver tree is a genuine conversation piece. Its lustrous, silky, coated leaves are 3 to 4 inches long and look like pure silver. They are sold as souvenir bookmarks in Cape Town, South Africa. This species is very particular about soil and exposure. It must have good drainage, and a coastal environment is strongly recommended.

Ligustrum lucidum
Glossy privet

Evergreen
Zones 8–10
Native to China, Korea, and Japan

Fast growing to 35–40 feet tall and 15–20 feet wide; round headed, often multitrunked

Its dense head; glossy, deep green foliage; and ability to take shearing make this a very popular hedge or screen plant. Feathery clusters of milky white flowers in summer are followed by heavy bunches of small, berrylike, blue-black fruits. This tree tolerates salt winds and a wide variety of soils. It is a good tree for areas where root space is restricted and makes a handsome container specimen. Glossy privet is useful as a small shade tree in a lawn or as a street tree, although the falling fruit may be messy.

Liquidambar styraciflua
American sweet gum

Deciduous
Zones 5–10
Native to the eastern and southern United States and Mexico
Moderate growing to 90 feet; a symmetrical pyramid when young, spreading and becoming irregular with maturity

The sweet gum is a reliable tree for autumn color. The star-shaped leaves, which resemble maple leaves, turn rich shades of crimson to purple in the fall. The color lasts as long as six weeks. The fruit, which matures in the fall, is the size of a golf ball and is prickly like a burr. It may be a nuisance when it drops. The corky ridges on the branches give this tree winter interest. It is a good skyline tree.

This tree will grow in a wide variety of sites, but does best in rich clay or loam soils. It is subject to chlorosis (yellowing of leaves) in heavy, alkaline soils; the addition of iron sulfate or chelates will help prevent this.

This tree does well in the home garden and is often used as a street tree.

The following cultivars are selected for fall color.

'Burgundy' has purplish fall leaves.

'Festival' is a narrow, upright tree with pink and orange fall color.

'Palo Alto' turns orange-red in the fall.

Liriodendron tulipifera (tulip tree, yellow poplar, tulip poplar)

Magnolia grandiflora (southern magnolia)

Liriodendron tulipifera

Tulip tree, yellow poplar, tulip poplar

Deciduous
Zones 5-9
Native to the eastern United States
Fast growing; some have grown 60-70 feet in 70 years; tall, pyramidal

This is the tallest of the eastern hardwoods and needs plenty of room to develop properly. Its beauty lies in its uniquely shaped, bright green leaves that create an attractive, light canopy. It can look like a very clean sycamore from a distance. The fall color is yellow. Large, tulip-shaped, greenish yellow flowers with an orange blotch at the base are borne in late spring. The flowers are best viewed up close, since they tend to blend into the foliage from a distance.

The wood of this tree has been found to be somewhat brittle, and the roots can be invasive. It does poorly in drought and alkaline soils. This tree is best used in open areas, parks, and golf courses; it is a good skyline tree and can be grown in a large lawn.

Sooty mold and honeydew from aphids can become a problem with this species. Do not use it over a patio or parking area for this reason.

'Fastigiatum' is a smaller cultivar that reaches only 35 feet and has a narrow, columnar form.

MAGNOLIA
MAGNOLIA

Magnolias can be either evergreen or deciduous. Among the deciduous are two types: those that bloom before the leaves come out and those that bloom after the leaves appear.

Magnolias are not difficult to grow. They will often do well in a suitably sheltered site even in climates one or two zones colder than the zone listed for the species. Some flowers may be lost, but the tree will survive.

Magnolia acuminata
Cucumber tree

Deciduous
Zones 4-8
Native to the eastern United States
Fast growing to 60-100 feet tall and half as wide

The most stately of the hardier magnolias, this is a vigorous tree that needs room to develop properly. It is primarily a shade tree; its flowers are relatively inconspicuous. Its common name is derived from the shape and color of its fruit clusters.

Magnolia × **'Elizabeth'**
Elizabeth magnolia

Deciduous
Zones 5-9
Hybrid of *M. heptapeta (M. denudata)* and *M. acuminata*
Fast growing to at least 45 feet

This tree has fuzzy, tapered buds that give it special winter interest. These open into large flowers of a soft, butter yellow, a rare color for a magnolia. The flowers come on in one large flush in the spring, usually 10 days later than the saucer magnolia, and therefore are safer from late frost. The tree continues to produce a few intermittent blooms throughout the summer. It also begins to bloom as a very young plant. This tree roots readily from cuttings.

Magnolia grandiflora
Southern magnolia

Evergreen
Zones 7-9
Native to the southern United States
Moderate growing to 60-75 feet tall and 35-55 feet wide

The southern magnolia is a legend in the southern United States. To see the large (8 inches or more), fragrant, creamy white flowers and lustrous, heavily textured, 5- to 8-inch-long leaves is to enjoy one of the finest flowering trees. Among the cultivars are 'St. Mary', a smaller tree (20 feet) known for its abundant bloom and predictable shape, and 'Edith Bogue', hardy to zone 6.

Magnolia × soulangiana (saucer magnolia)

Magnolia stellata (star magnolia)

Magnolia macrophylla
Bigleaf magnolia

Deciduous
Zones 6-9
Native to a small section
of West Virginia and along
the Kentucky–Virginia and
Tennessee–North Carolina
borders
Moderate growing to 20-40
feet and half as wide with
a round, open top

This tree has the largest leaves
of any native tree. They are 20
to 30 inches long with stalks
and are formed like earlobes at
the base. The bigleaf magnolia
has a luxuriant tropical look,
but because wind tears and
breaks the leaves and makes
the tree look battered, its use is
limited to that of a novelty in
well-protected spots.

Creamy white, fragrant
flowers, 8 to 12 inches across
with numerous stamens, appear in July. Rose-colored
cucumberlike pods split to re-
veal red seeds in early fall.
This species grows best in
slightly acidic soils.

Magnolia × soulangiana
Saucer magnolia

Deciduous
Zones 6-9
Hybrid of two species native
to China
Moderate growing to about
20-30 feet tall and often
equally wide

The saucer magnolia may be
the most widely planted and
best-known magnolia. It is a
very popular photographic subject. It blooms even while still
small, and flower colors of the
different varieties range from
white to dark reddish purple.
Saucer magnolias are sometimes planted where a more
erect-growing tree should have
been placed; allow the space
needed for development of normal shape and form.

This is a hardy tree and
should not be planted in a spot
open to the warm winter sun.
This may rush the flowers'
development and make them

susceptible to late frost damage. As for foliage, saucer
magnolias are not among the
best-looking magnolias after
the flowers have faded.

Magnolia stellata
Star magnolia

Deciduous
Zones 5-9
Native to Japan
Moderate growing to 25 feet
with a rounded habit

This tree is a beautiful sight
when the fragrant white flowers with strap-shaped petals
appear before the leaves in late
winter or early spring. The
flowers can be damaged by
frost, so avoid southern expo-
sures that encourage buds to
develop early and flowers
to open too fast. This hardy,
small, and attractive tree
makes a good specimen plant.

Magnolia virginiana
Sweetbay magnolia

Deciduous or evergreen
Zones 5-9
Native to the southern and
eastern United States

In the northern United States
grows to 10-20 feet; in the
southern states can reach
40-60 feet

The sweetbay magnolia grows
as an evergreen in the South,
but it is also one of the most
popular magnolias in the colder
areas, where it develops into a
tall, deciduous shrub. It suggests a miniature version of
the southern magnolia with its
smaller, fragrant, creamy
white, globular flowers and
smaller (5-inch) leaves, glossy
above, blue-white beneath. It
blooms from late spring to
early fall in favorable growing
sites. Being native to lowlands,
it prefers rich, moist soil. This
is a good small urban tree.

MALUS
CRAB APPLE

More than 600 species and
varieties of flowering crab apples grow in the United States
and Canada. It is the most
widely adapted of the flowering trees. Like all hardy flowering fruit trees, it requires a
period of winter chilling and is
not adapted to the mild-winter

Malus floribunda (Japanese flowering crab apple)

Malus 'Red Jade' (Red Jade crab apple)

Melaleuca linariifolia (flaxleaf paperbark, snow-in-summer)

areas of the Deep South and southern California.

In some localities crab apples are vulnerable to apple scab and other stresses. In fact, some of the most popular species have been proven to be most susceptible to insect and disease problems. Noteworthy among these are 'Almey', 'Flame', 'Eleyi', and 'Hopa'. Varieties that are resistant to scab, cedar apple rust, mildew, and fire blight have been developed. Those listed here are resistant to disease, blossom annually, and bear small, attractive fruit that hangs on the tree well into the winter or until it is eaten by birds.

Malus baccata
Siberian crab apple

Deciduous
Zones 2–9
Native to Manchuria and China
Grows to 15–30 feet; vase shaped

This tree is a heavy bearer, and the fruit is usable and

attractive to wildlife. Fragrant, white flowers in early spring are followed by the 1-inch-diameter fruit. This tree is reasonably disease resistant.

Malus 'Donald Wyman'
Donald Wyman crab apple

Deciduous
Zones 4–8
Hybrid of undetermined crosses
Moderate growing to 30–40 feet

This is a relatively large, upright crab apple with shiny, leathery leaves. It has pure white flowers, which are followed by persistent small, red fruit. This is a good street tree and is suitable for use under utility wires.

Malus floribunda
Japanese flowering crab apple

Deciduous
Zones 5–8
Native to Japan
Grows to 20 feet with a graceful, arching spread

Deep pink buds are pinkish white in full flower and are followed by small reddish yellow fruit. Japanese flowering crab apple blooms profusely. It is resistant to scab but will get some fire blight.

Malus 'Red Jade'
Red Jade crab apple

Deciduous
Zones 4–8
Hybrid of undetermined crosses
Slow growing to 15–20 feet

'Red Jade' gets its name from the color of its fruit. Small, white flowers appear in great profusion on long, irregular, weeping branches in the spring. The heavy yield of usable fruit lasts late into the fall. This species is reasonably disease resistant, but will get some scab.

Malus sargentii
Sargent crab apple

Deciduous
Zones 4–8
Native to Japan
Slow growing to 15 feet

The sargent crab apple has profuse clusters of small, fragrant, white flowers. These are followed by masses of small, dark red fruit. This is a dwarf, spreading variety of crab apple with good disease resistance. It blooms and bears best in alternate years. The cultivar 'Jewelberry' is an annual bloomer.

Melaleuca linariifolia
Flaxleaf paperbark, snow-in-summer

Evergreen
Zones 9, 10
Native to Australia
Slow to moderate growing to 30 feet; narrow, upright, open when young; denser and round headed with age

Small, thin, pale beige branches, with clusters of delicately pointed blue-green leaves, form an elegant contrast to the honey brown papery bark peeling on the trunk and older limbs of this tree.

Metasequoia glyptostroboides (dawn redwood)

Nyssa sylvatica (black tupelo, black gum, sour gum, pepperidge)

In all seasons it is distinguished by its stylized texture and subtle coloring. Flaxleaf paperbark becomes truly spectacular in early summer when it is in full bloom, giving the effect of new-fallen snow. This species was thought to be extinct until it was rediscovered in the 1940s. It is a good urban tree and is used widely in southern Korean cities.

Melia azedarach
Chinaberry

Deciduous
Zones 7–10
Native to Asia
Fast growing to 30–40 feet and equally wide; spreading, umbrellalike crown

This tree is useful where most trees won't grow and so is a valuable tree for desert regions. Its purple flowers are followed by poisonous yellow berries. It also sprouts suckers, drops berries, and has weak wood. 'Umbraculifera', the Texas umbrella tree, is more common than the species. It

has a tighter, more rounded, umbrellalike form and is used in the desert.

Metasequoia glyptostroboides
Dawn redwood

Deciduous
Zones 5–8
Native to China
Fast growing to 80–100 feet

The dawn redwood is a fossil-age conifer that resembles the deciduous bald cypress in foliage character, although its flat needles are closer in size to those of the hemlock, which is a northern tree. The trunk shape differs from that of the bald cypress considerably. Dawn redwood has a buttress-shaped trunk, very wide at the base with deeply fluted bark that develops with age. Its structure has a regular appearance with horizontal, pendulous branches.

The bark on larger branches is reddish brown and the twig bark somewhat orange-brown. The summer foliage color is light green, turning yellow in the fall.

Nyssa sylvatica
Black tupelo, black gum, sour gum, pepperidge

Deciduous
Zones 4–9
Native to the eastern United States
Moderate growing to 30–50 feet tall and about half as wide

In the wild, this tree grows along riverbanks and on floodplains. Its lovely orange or scarlet autumn leaves stand out against the foliage of evergreens.

Black tupelo develops a dense canopy of beautiful, glossy, deep green foliage. The spring buds make a bright red patch in the woods, and in winter the bare branches form an attractive silhouette against the sky. This tree should be transplanted young to ensure success.

Olea europaea
Olive

Evergreen
Zones 9, 10
Native to the Mediterranean countries and western Asia
Fairly fast growing in youth, slowing down with age, to 20–30 feet; rounded head

The olive's attractive, gnarled gray trunk and gray-green leaves with silvery undersides are seen throughout California. The olive is one of the easier trees to transplant when it is mature.

If the fruit is not to be consumed, it is a nuisance when it drops on paving or any trafficked area. The fallen fruit will harm a lawn and must be raked up. Scale is sometimes a problem on olives.

Several cultivars are available. 'Swan Hill' is fruitless, so it makes a desirable street tree on wide avenues. 'Ascolano' is the most attractive fruiting variety and is grown commercially. The large fruit is tender and should be handled with care if it is to be preserved.

Oxydendrum arboreum
(sourwood, sorrel tree)

Paulownia tomentosa (empress tree)

Phellodendron amurense
(amur corktree)

'Manzanillo' has a stiffer branching habit than 'Ascolano' and is less desirable for home planting. Its large fruit is good for oil and for preserving and is not as easily damaged as that of 'Ascolano'.

Ostrya virginiana
American hop hornbeam

Deciduous
Zones 4-9
Native to eastern North America
Slow growing to 30-35 feet; round headed

This small, graceful tree has little problem with pests or diseases. The attractive bark of the trunk and larger branches has long, frayed, platelike strips. The foliage is medium green, developing a reddish autumn color. American hop hornbeam is tolerant of a wide range of soils and it does quite well under adverse city conditions.

Oxydendrum arboreum
Sourwood, sorrel tree

Deciduous
Zones 5-9
Native to the eastern United States
Slow growing to 30-40 feet; pyramidal

The sourwood is considered by many to be one of the most beautiful native American small flowering trees. It is attractive the year around, starting with the translucent amber red of the young leaves as they unfold in the spring, continuing with the big, pendulous sprays of white flowers borne for a long period in July, and finishing with the brilliant scarlet color of the foliage in autumn. The sourwood is a light and feathery tree. Its delicate and enduring beauty is best enjoyed at close hand near a terrace or patio. It requires acid soil. The common name, sourwood, comes from its very sour-tasting foliage.

Parrotia persica
Persian parrotia

Deciduous
Zones 6-8
Native to Iran
Slow growing to 30-40 feet tall and 15-30 feet wide; oval habit with upsweeping branches

Persian parrotia is an excellent, pest-free, small specimen tree. It is colorful in all seasons but most spectacular in the fall when the dark green leaves turn from bright yellow to orange and finally to scarlet. In the winter the attractive bark is flaky with white patches beneath. The new spring leaves are reddish purple as they unfold.

Paulownia tomentosa
Empress tree

Deciduous
Zones 6-9
Native to China; naturalized in the southeastern United States
Fast growing to 40-60 feet tall and equally wide, with a rounded head

The spectacular empress tree thrives in full sun and rich, well-drained soil. It tolerates air pollution but does not do well in hot, dry conditions.

Vanilla-scented, pale violet flowers appear before the leaves, usually in April. The flowers are 2 inches long, trumpet shaped, and held in 1-foot-long clusters. If temperatures are very warm or very cold the tree does not flower well. This is a good tree where there is plenty of space, as in a park. If branched low, the dense shade this species creates makes it almost impossible to grow grass or other plants underneath.

Phellodendron amurense
Amur corktree

Deciduous
Zones 4-7
Native to China and Japan
Moderate growing to 30-50 feet tall with an even wider spread

The amur corktree has glossy, foot-long, dark green, compound leaves. The bark develops an attractive and unusual corky texture that is gray-black in color.

This tree is pest free and tolerant of both pollution and drought. The shallow root system precludes its use along

Picea abies (Norway spruce)

Picea glauca (white spruce)

streets or in lawns, but it makes a good light-shade tree, especially suited to parks or other large areas.

PICEA
SPRUCE

Most of the spruces of North America are native to the northern areas of the continent: Canada, Alaska, and the northern parts of the United States from Minnesota and Wisconsin to New England. Spruce trees can be identified and differentiated from other evergreens by their needles. The needles (leaves) of nearly all spruces are squarish in cross section and can be rolled between the thumb and index finger. Fir and hemlock needles are flattish and do not roll easily. Spruce cones also differ from those of fir. They hang downward rather than standing straight up and remain intact when they fall, rather than shattering.

Spruce mites, red spider mites, and the Cooley spruce gall adelgids are common pests. The mites are dark green to black or red, produce copious amounts of webbing, and turn the tree grayish. Cooley spruce gall adelgids cause conelike galls to form at the ends of twigs. Galls are green to reddish purple in spring, then turn brown, dry, and hard in summer. Check with a local garden center for ways to control these pests.

Picea abies
Norway spruce

Evergreen
Zones 3–8
Native to Europe
Fast growing and columnar to 100–150 feet

The Norway spruce is the most widely adapted spruce. Unlike many others, it is not a North American native and was brought from Europe.

These beautiful pyramidal evergreens grow more attractive as they age. Their branchlets gradually become more pendulous, and the trees naturally retain their lower branches and needles. This tree also bears very large (for a spruce) and attractive seed-bearing cones, 4 to 7 inches long.

Norway spruce makes an excellent windbreak and tall screen. Where space permits, this is also a good landscape specimen. It should not be planted on poor sites; avoid dry ridges and slopes where soils are likely to be low in fertility. This species prefers cool and moist locations. Hot weather weakens the tree.

Many unusual forms, varieties, or cultivars of the Norway spruce have been named. These range from dwarf to weeping and from compact to spreading. Many, especially the weeping forms, may require staking to bring them up to the desired height.

Picea glauca
White spruce

Evergreen
Zones 3, 4
Native to Alaska, Canada, and the northern United States

Moderate growing to 50–80 feet; conical with drooping branchlets

The white spruce is extremely hardy, withstanding both very cold and very hot, dry conditions. Although it is a large tree, there are two popular compact forms. 'Densata', Black Hills spruce, is slow growing. 'Conica' has a formal character and is also slow growing.

Picea omorika
Serbian spruce

Evergreen
Zones 4–8
Native to southern Europe
Moderate growth to 60–100 feet with a columnar, slender habit and upturned branch tips

This is a narrow, spirelike spruce with glossy, dark green needles borne on a slender trunk with short, ascending branches. It has a very narrow, pyramidal head. This tree usually retains its lower branches, a valuable trait in a specimen tree that is expected to retain

Picea pungens (Colorado spruce)

Pinus aristata (bristlecone pine)

its beauty throughout its lifetime. No spruce of this height is likely to cover less ground area. This fact permits this species to be used in small landscapes where other spruces would not be suitable.

Picea orientalis
Oriental spruce

Evergreen
Zones 5–8
Native to Asia Minor
Slow growing to 80 feet in a narrow spire

This is one of the best spruces for use in areas where summers are hot and dry. It is a neat tree with graceful branches and very short, ¼- to ½-inch needles of a deep, glossy green. Its cones are 2 to 4 inches long, reddish purple at first, brown when mature.

    This tree makes a fine specimen or windbreak, but its foliage may brown in colder climates. It is very tolerant of heat and drought but may be vulnerable to spruce budworm where that is a problem.

Picea pungens
Colorado spruce

Evergreen
Zones 3–8
Native to Wyoming, Utah, Colorado, and New Mexico
Slow to moderate growing to 80–100 feet; stiff, pyramidal form with dense, horizontal branches

As a young tree, the Colorado spruce is beautiful and vigorous. Its growth slows with age, and it has a tendency to lose its lower branches, which detracts from its beauty as a mature tree. Nurseries propagate several forms. Common among these are 'Koster' with silver needles; 'Moerheimii' with waxy, silver blue needles; and 'Hoopsii' with very silvery foliage. 'Glauca' is the most widely sold cultivar. Its foliage is gray-blue; new growth is light blue. 'Glauca' is very drought resistant.

Picea sitchensis
Sitka spruce

Evergreen
Zones 6–9
Native from Alaska to California
Fast growing to 100–150 feet; develops from a conical shape to a broad pyramid

Sitka spruce is a massive tree—the tallest known spruce and a very rapid grower. It grows best in cool and humid coastal climates and is generally long-lived.

PINUS
PINE

Of the more than 100 species of pines worldwide, more than 40 are native to North America. These evergreens vary widely, from slow-growing trees suitable for container planting to the picturesque, wind-shaped pines of the Pacific Coast, to the majestic hardy pines of the northern forests. Some are used in patio planters and shaped into bonsai trees. In the garden they are valuable as shade trees, as specimen trees, as windbreaks, and as tall hedges.

    The individual species of pine are identified by the size and number of needles that are held in each bundle and by the appearance of the cones.

Pinus aristata
Bristlecone pine

Evergreen
Zones 5–7
Native to the mountains of the western United States
Very slow growing to 45 feet

The needles on this tree are five in a bundle, 1 to 1½ inches long, and usually flecked with white dots of resin. They will remain on twigs 20 to 30 years, giving the ends of the branches a bushy or brushlike appearance. The cones are 3½ inches long. A bristlecone pine may grow only 3 inches in height per year, on average. Some specimens in the mountains of the southwestern United States are almost five thousand years old—the oldest living trees in the world. These trees will grow on very dry and exposed sites. Use this small and picturesque pine as a specimen, in a rock garden, or as a container plant where years will pass before it outgrows its space.

Pinus densiflora (Japanese red pine)

Pinus nigra (Austrian pine)

Pinus densiflora
Japanese red pine

Evergreen
Zones 5-9
Native to Japan, China,
and Korea
Fast growing to 50-60 feet and
equally wide

The Japanese red pine often
forms two or more trunks at
ground level and has attractive, reddish bark. The
branches spread horizontally,
and the tree has an open, loose
habit. It can be dwarfed. Many
cultivars with interesting
forms are available.

Pinus echinata
Shortleaf pine

Evergreen
Zones 6-9
Native to New York through
Florida and to Texas
Grows to 100 feet

The needles of the shortleaf
pine are held two in a bundle,
sometimes three on young
trees, and are 3 to 5 inches
long. The cones are 1½ to 2
inches long.

This pine is widespread
throughout the southeastern
United States. It grows in
coastal plains, piedmont areas,
and in the mountains up to
2,000 feet in elevation; growth
is poor above 2,000 feet. The
shortleaf pine grows naturally
in dense stands and will do
well in a variety of soils. It has
been extensively planted in reforestation projects. It is sometimes available as a container
plant for landscaping and
makes a handsome lawn tree.

Pinus lambertiana
Sugar pine

Evergreen
Zones 6, 7
Native to Oregon through Baja
California
Slow growing for the first
5 years; eventually grows
to 200 feet or more

This is the world's tallest pine.
Older trees are usually flat
topped with an open, spreading
head. The blue-green needles
are 3 to 4 inches long and held
in bundles of five. The cones
are 12 to 20 inches long. Sugar

pine becomes more beautiful
with age, and it is a good specimen tree.

Pinus nigra
Austrian pine

Evergreen
Zones 4-8
Native to central and southern
Europe and Asia Minor
Moderate growing to 60-80 feet
in height, but can grow to 100
feet; at maturity it becomes
flat topped, but is densely
pyramidal and wide spreading
in youth

The sharp, stiff needles of Austrian pine are held two in a
bundle and are 4 to 8 inches
long. The oval cones grow to
about 3 inches long.

This is an important pine in
the eastern United States and
Canada. It is tolerant of moist,
but not wet, soils and city conditions and can be used as a
specimen tree or as a screen. It
will withstand winter cold and
wind. This species is vulnerable to tip blight where springs
are wet.

Pinus parviflora
Japanese white pine

Evergreen
Zones 6, 7
Native to Japan
Slow growing to 90 feet

The needles of the Japanese
white pine are five in a bundle
and are 1½ to 2½ inches long.
The cones are 2 to 3 inches
long and can remain on the
tree for six to seven years.
The crown of this tree can
spread almost as wide as the
tree is tall, so it should be
given ample room to develop.
This is an excellent specimen
tree that could be more widely
used. It grows on sandy loam to
silty clay.

'Glauca', silver Japanese
white pine, has needles that
are silver blue. This tree is
considered to be more striking
than the species.

Pinus pungens
Table Mountain pine

Evergreen
Zones 5-8
Native to New Jersey through
Georgia
Slow growing to 20-50 feet

Pinus radiata (Monterey pine)

Pinus strobus (white pine)

Pinus sylvestris (Scotch pine, Scots pine)

The stiff, dark green needles of the Table Mountain pine are held on spreading branches that often form an irregular or flat-topped crown. The needles are 2 to 3 inches long and are held two or three in a bundle. The 3- to 4-inch cones stay on the tree for several years. This scrub pine does well in a large container.

Pinus radiata
Monterey pine

Evergreen
Zones 8–10
Native to California through Baja California
Fast growing to 60–100 feet

The 3- to 7-inch needles are held two or three in a bundle. Clusters of 3- to 5-inch cones stay on the tree for many years. The Monterey pine is normally pyramidal but develops a rounded, flattish crown with age and is often contorted by the wind. Use it for windbreaks, tall screens, and hedges on large properties.

Pinus strobus
White pine

Evergreen
Zones 2–8
Native to eastern North America
Fast growing to 150 feet

The needles of the white pine are five in a bundle and 3 to 5 inches long. The cones are 4 to 5 inches long. In the forest, this pine has been known to reach 200 feet tall. White pine does best in well-drained sandy loams or silty soils, but it will grow in most soils. This long-lived tree can survive 450 years or more. In the southern Appalachian mountains it grows at elevations of up to 4,000 feet or higher. This tree has been widely planted in reforestation projects and as an ornamental; it is often used as a screen. It is very susceptible to air pollution, however, and should not be used in urban sites. A number of horticultural selections have been developed for special planting situations. The following are two of the most common cultivars.

'Nana', dwarf white pine, is very compact and grows 6 to 10 feet tall with a spread of 10 feet or more.

'Pendula', weeping white pine, has branches that droop and touch the ground.

Pinus sylvestris
Scotch pine, Scots pine

Evergreen
Zones 3–8
Native to Eurasia
Grows to 75 feet

The twisted, green needles of the Scotch pine are borne two in a bundle and are 1½ to 3 inches long. The cones are 2 inches long. The bark is reddish orange at first, maturing to a grayish red-brown. Scotch pines are planted as Christmas trees and specimen trees. This is a variable species, and many strains and cultivars have been developed.

Pinus taeda
Loblolly pine

Evergreen
Zones 7–9
Native to New Jersey through Texas
Fast growing to 100 feet

The needles of this tree come three in a bundle and are 6 to 8 inches long. This species has been widely planted as a source of timber and pulpwood. When grown in the open, this tree develops a good crown and makes an excellent shade tree. The loblolly pine grows quite well in poorly drained soils. It does not do well in dry or sandy locations.

Pinus thunbergiana
Japanese black pine

Evergreen
Zones 5–8
Native to Japan
Fast growing to 90 feet

The needles of this tree are borne two in a cluster and are 3 to 4 inches long. The cones are 2 to 3 inches long. The crown becomes irregular and spreading as it approaches maturity. Large, white terminal buds help to identify this tree. It is tolerant of salt spray and is one of the best evergreens for seashore and highway plantings.

Pistacia chinensis (Chinese pistachio)

Pittosporum tobira (Japanese pittosporum, mock orange)

Podocarpus macrophyllus (yew pine)

Pistacia chinensis
Chinese pistachio

Deciduous
Zones 6–10
Native to China
Moderate growing to 50–60 feet tall and equally wide; spreading, umbrellalike crown

This is one of the best trees for filtered shade. The bright green leaves grow up to 12 inches in length and are divided into fine-textured leaflets. The new leaves have a pink tinge, turning brilliant shades of yellow to orange and red in the fall. The zigzag branching pattern of this species is quite attractive.

Widely adapted, Chinese pistachio grows best with summer heat. This is an excellent lawn or street tree, although female trees will produce berries when a male tree is nearby. There are no disease problems. Because of its uneven growth habit, a little extra pruning may be needed when the tree is young to develop good form.

PITTOSPORUM
PITTOSPORUM

Pittosporums fall into two groups: the hedge-forming plants and those species that are best left standing alone. Species vary in the size, shape, and color of their leaves and the resulting texture of the canopy. Only the tree types are discussed here.

Pittosporum rhombifolium
Queensland pittosporum

Evergreen
Zones 9, 10
Native to eastern Australia
Moderate to fast growing to 20–35 feet

This pittosporum has diamond-shaped, 4-inch-long, glossy green leaves and showy fruit. It is often used as a screen.

Pittosporum tobira
Japanese pittosporum, mock orange

Evergreen
Zones 8–10
Native to China and Japan
Slow growing to 18 feet

This durable plant is better known as a foundation shrub, but it can be coaxed upward on one or several trunks to a patio-sized tree. Small, sweetly fragrant, off-white flowers are produced in profusion throughout the spring.

Platanus × acerifolia
London plane tree

Deciduous
Zones 5–9
Hybrid of *P. occidentalis* and *P. orientalis*
Fast growing to 40–60 feet; open, spreading crown

This versatile and widely adapted tree can take harsh city conditions, drought, and tough soils. It is often pollarded—a severe pruning technique (see page 27). The London plane tree is widely used as a street tree and in malls. The large-lobed leaves are bright green; the brown, ball-shaped fruit is borne two to a cluster. Many consider its striking green and white flaking bark the most attractive feature of this tree. In the fall the foliage turns yellow-brown. Of all the members of the Sycamore family, this is the most resistant to anthracnose. Especially resistant cultivars are 'Bloodgood', 'Columbia', and 'Liberty'.

Podocarpus macrophyllus
Yew pine

Evergreen
Zones 8–10
Native to Japan
Slow growing to 50–60 feet; erect, columnar form

Yew pine is a valuable indoor or outdoor plant with a graceful oriental character. Long, narrow, rather stiff, bright green leaves grow on slightly drooping branches. It is pest free and widely adapted, but it may show chlorosis in alkaline or heavy soils. Protected locations will extend its hardiness. It is a good tree to plant along entryways or for use in containers; it also makes a fine hedge or espalier.

POPULUS
POPLAR

Few trees hardy in temperate zones grow as rapidly as

Populus nigra 'Italica' (Lombardy poplar)

Prosopis glandulosa var. *torreyana* (mesquite)

poplars. An unrooted cutting, spring-planted in an area of rich soil and abundant moisture, can reach 12 feet or more in height by the following autumn. Although such significant growth slows down as the tree grows older, it is still unique among hardy trees. This rapid growth rate, coupled with tolerance of a wide variety of soil types and the production of wood with industrial value, have led to considerable interest in poplars for reforestation.

In some very arid areas of the West, locally native poplars are among the few trees that will survive and grow large enough to provide shade. Of these adapted species, male trees that do not produce clouds of cottonlike seed, such as 'Siouxland', the cottonless cottonwood, are much preferred over ordinary seedlings. Another important use for poplars, particularly the narrow, upright varieties, is for quick-growing screening to hide unsightly areas and buildings or to make windbreaks. When there is enough room, the ideal solution to a screening problem is to plant a row of the very rapid growing but short-lived Lombardy poplars adjacent to a row of arbovitae, spruce, or narrow junipers. When these poplars begin to decline, the evergreens will be tall enough to do the screening job.

Populus alba
White poplar

Deciduous
Zones 4–10
Native to Europe and Asia
Rapid growing to 50–90 feet

This tall and wide-spreading species is very hardy. Its foliage is among the prettiest of all poplars. The leaves resemble small maple leaves, dark green above and silvery white underneath; they are especially attractive on a breezy day. White poplar grows exceptionally well at the seashore, being highly resistant to salt spray and even temporary immersion of the root area. Its major drawback is the persistent sprouting of shoots from its wide-spreading root system.

'Pyramidalis' ('Bolleana') has the fine foliage of the white poplar but is better suited for screening purposes because it does not sprout from the roots as the species does.

Populus nigra 'Italica'
Lombardy poplar

Deciduous
Zones 2–6
Native to southern Europe
Fast growing to 90 feet; columnar

The handsome Lombardy poplar is one of the oldest known varieties of ornamental trees. It is highly useful as a tall screen or accent tree in every respect but one—it is very susceptible to stem canker disease as it reaches maturity. There is great variation in disease incidence, but generally Lombardy poplars grow better and healthier the farther north they are planted. There are some places where they do exceptionally well. Elsewhere, the tree is still useful for "instant screening," with the knowledge that there may be

disease losses after 15 to 20 years of vigorous growth.

Populus nigra var. *thevestina,* Theves poplar or Algerian poplar, is a similar variety that is more canker resistant. It has white bark and grows broader than the Lombardy poplar.

Populus simonii 'Fastigiata'

Deciduous
Zones 2–6
Native to China
Fast growing to 35 feet; narrow, pyramidal

This attractive, narrow tree is a variety of one of the most hardy of all poplars, from the harsh climate of northern China. It has pretty, reddish branchlets bearing shiny, bright green leaves. It reaches approximately 45 feet in height at maturity and, although not as narrow as the Lombardy poplar, it is still much taller than it is broad. It makes a fine, quick-growing screen plant and is resistant to canker disease, so is quite long-lived. Also, it does not sucker from the roots.

Prunus avium (sweet cherry, Mazzard cherry)

Prunus laurocerasus (cherry-laurel)

Prosopis glandulosa var. torreyana
Mesquite

Deciduous
Zones 7–9
Native to the southwestern United States
Grows to 30 feet with a loose-spreading crown; usually multitrunked

This is a tree for hot, dry regions. Its gray-green foliage casts filtered shade, and its greenish yellow flowers in spring and summer attract bees. Mesquite is drought tolerant and takes alkaline soils. It can be used as a screen or windbreak.

PRUNUS

This genus comprises over 400 species and numerous cultivars that grow in temperate climates, mostly in the Northern Hemisphere.

Included are all the stone fruits: almonds, apricots, cherries, nectarines, peaches, and plums. These fruit trees are grown for their edible fruits and, in many cases, are also highly ornamental. The species

included here are divided into three groups: the cherries, the plums, and the evergreen laurels.

CHERRIES

The cherries fall into three groups: the European, the American, and the Asian. Cherries are not tolerant of anaerobic soil conditions, so they should not be planted in very wet or heavy clay soils. In general, the Asian types are less hardy than the others.

Prunus avium
Sweet cherry, Mazzard cherry

Deciduous
Zones 4–8
Native to Europe and Asia
Fast growing to 50 feet

Sweet cherries have been cultivated for two and a half centuries, and this species is the ancestor of most sweet cherries. Its attractive bark matures to mahogany red. This tree is wide spreading with flowers produced singly or in 3- to 5-flowered clusters along the

sides of the branches. The fruit is juicy and edible. 'Plena' is a cultivar with roselike white, double flowers.

Prunus laurocerasus
Cherry-laurel

Evergreen
Zones 6–8
Native to southeastern Europe
Moderate to fast growing; can be trained to multiple stems or single stem; fountainlike form as wide as it is tall

This is an excellent landscape plant for the South. Its varieties range from ground covers to small trees. They thrive in many difficult situations, from full sun to dense shade, and in all but the most dry or alkaline soil. Cherry-laurel is often used for screening or for clipped or natural hedges.

The lustrous, bright green leaves are 4 to 6 inches long and have a leathery texture. The fragrant flowers bloom in white, terminal spikes in May. If trimmed, however, this species will not bloom. Fruit clusters turn from red to black and attract birds until early winter.

Many cultivars are available. 'Schipkaensis' is hardier (to zone 5) and is a good choice for more northern regions. 'Otto Luyken' is hardier, too, and more compact.

Prunus 'Okame'
Okame flowering cherry

Deciduous
Zones 5–9
Hybrid of *P. campanulata* and *P. incisa*
Moderate to fast growing, 20–30 feet tall and almost as wide

This ornamental hybrid blooms even when young. In early spring, deep-maroon buds open into a profusion of small, bright crimson-rose flowers that last for two weeks, longer than many cherries. The tree is vigorous, upright, and branching. Its fine-textured foliage is dark green in summer and turns shades of yellow, orange, and red in fall.

Prunus sargentii
Sargent cherry

Deciduous
Zones 5–9

Prunus serrulata (Japanese flowering cherry)

Prunus subhirtella (higan cherry)

Prunus yedoensis (yoshino cherry)

Native to northern Japan, Korea, and the Sakhalin peninsula
Moderate growing to 50 feet

This is the hardiest of the Asian cherries. The pink flowers bloom before the double Japanese cherries. This beautiful tree is long-lived, has good fall color and attractive bark, and matures into one of the largest Asian cherries.

Prunus serotina
Black cherry

Deciduous
Zones 4–9
Native to Nova Scotia through North Dakota and south to Florida and Texas
Moderate growing to 90 feet

This North American native has fragrant, white flowers in clusters 2 to 6 inches long. The fruit is black and generally not favored by people but is especially relished by birds. When grown in the open as a specimen, this tree develops a huge, rounded crown. The branches are partially drooping. The black cherry is a good timber tree but is considered a weedy and undesirable landscape tree in some areas. It is best planted in a natural environment, away from buildings and patios.

Prunus serrulata
Japanese flowering cherry

Deciduous
Zones 6–9
Native to eastern Asia
Grows to 20–25 feet

The attractive habit of this cherry is further enhanced when the fragrant, white, double flowers bloom in the spring. It is one of the two most common types of cherries in the famous Washington, D.C., plantings.

More than 120 cultivars of this species have been developed. 'Amanogawa' grows to 20 feet and is the most narrow and upright of the Japanese cherries. Its flowers are pale pink. 'Kwanzan', considered stiff and unattractive by some, is among the most popular and hardy of the double-flowered Asian cherries. It grows to 12 to 18 feet and has deep-pink flowers.

Prunus subhirtella
Higan cherry

Deciduous
Zones 6–8
Native to Japan
Grows to 25 feet tall and equally wide

Higan cherry blooms early in the spring with a large, showy display of pink flowers. 'Autumnalis' is a semidouble pale pink form that blooms sporadically during warm spells in the late autumn and winter and then blooms again more heavily in the early spring. 'Pendula' has a graceful, weeping form with single, pale pink blossoms.

Prunus yedoensis
Yoshino cherry

Deciduous
Zones 6–8
Hybrid of *P. serrulata* and *P. subhirtella*
Fast growing to 40 feet; flat topped, wide spreading

Yoshino cherry is one of the most rapid-growing cherries.

Its single white flowers are borne in abundance early in the season. This is the predominant tree in the flowering cherry display in the Washington, D.C., tidal basin.

PLUMS

The plums, like cherries, include three varieties: North American, European, and Asiatic. Most plums are heavy spring bloomers, and some furnish abundant edible fruit. Plum trees can be small trees or shrubs—they seldom exceed 30 feet in height. Some plums also form thickets.

Among the flowering plums, some bear edible fruit annually; others bear rarely or not at all and are selected for their foliage and flowers. Appropriate species can be chosen depending on placement. Near sidewalks, fruit drop can be annoying. Where the fruit can be picked, fruiting varieties are appreciated. A number of plum species require two seedling trees or two different varieties for cross-pollination to obtain a good set of fruit.

Prunus cerasifera (cherry plum)

Prunus caroliniana (Carolina cherry-laurel)

Pseudotsuga menziesii
(Douglas fir)

Prunus cerasifera
Cherry plum

Deciduous
Zones 4–8
Native to central Asia through
the Balkans
Grows to 25 feet tall and
equally wide

Cherry plum flowers are white,
and the yellow or reddish fruit
is quite sweet. The cultivars
'Atropurpurea' and 'Thunder-
cloud' are purple-leaf forms.

EVERGREEN LAURELS

The cherry-laurels, or laurel-
cherries, are grown for their
attractive evergreen foliage.
The fruit is small and is eaten
by birds. These plants are used
as hedges, screens, back-
grounds, and specimens.

Prunus caroliniana
Carolina cherry-laurel

Evergreen
Zones 7–10
Native to North Carolina
through Texas
Fast growing to 18–40 feet

Cherry-laurel is a large shrub
or a small tree that often forms
a dense thicket. The trunk
diameter can reach 1 foot. The
flowers are white. The plant
has been widely dispersed by
birds who eat the ½-inch black
fruit. This species is relatively
free from insects and disease
and can stand heavy shearing.

Prunus lusitanica
Portugal laurel

Evergreen
Zones 7–9
Native to Spain, Portugal, and
the Canary Islands
Slow growing to 40 feet

This is a beautiful specimen
when allowed to develop naturally. The small, white flowers
are held in clusters to 10
inches in length. The fruit is
red, turning dark purple. Portugal laurel is hardier than
many other laurels and will
withstand sun, heat, and wind.
   A number of cultivars have
been developed, such as
'Myrtifolia', with smaller foliage, and 'Variegata', the
leaves of which are streaked
with white markings.

Pseudolarix kaempferi
Golden-larch

Deciduous conifer
Zones 4–7
Native to eastern China
Moderate growing to 40–70
feet tall and almost as wide

This beautiful tree is breathtaking in its brief autumn
splendor and prized for its
graceful, spreading, pyramidal
shape. The feathery foliage, 1½
to 2 inches long and borne in
bunches, is also attractive
in spring and summer, giving
light shade.
   This is a fine specimen tree
where space permits, and it
makes a good screen. The unusual 3-inch cones grow upright above the branches and
are attractive in summer
and early fall. The bark is a
handsome reddish brown. This
tree likes full sun and deep,
moist soil. In its northern range
it needs protection from the
wind. Unlike other larches, it is
pest free.

Pseudotsuga menziesii
Douglas fir

Needled evergreen
Zones 4–9
Native to Alaska through the
western United States into
Mexico
Fast growing to 200 feet tall,
but usually less, and 30–60
feet wide

The Douglas fir is unmatched
as a timber tree. It produces
more lumber than any other
single species in the United
States. It also makes an attractive landscape tree. When
young, its uniform pyramidal
shape makes it an ideal Christmas tree.
   Stiff branches droop on the
lower part of this tree, but
the upper branches extend upward and outward. Soft, flat,
bluish green needles are arranged in a spiral on the twigs.
The new growth in spring is an
attractive apple green. The foliage is always fragrant and
fresh smelling.
   The Douglas fir is native to
a wide range of habitats, so select plants grown from a seed

Pyrus calleryana (callery pear)

Quercus agrifolia (coast live oak)

source that best matches local conditions. The mature size of this tree varies with available moisture. When grown in areas with a high water table, the roots may spread close to the surface rather than growing deep down into the ground. When this happens, the roots of a 60-foot tree, for example, may only be 12 to 18 inches deep. Many times, in new housing developments, areas are cleared, leaving just a few trees around the homes. If the roots are shallow, these trees may blow over in the first big wind because they no longer have the mutual support and protection of other trees.

PYRUS
ORNAMENTAL PEAR

Members of this genus can be either deciduous or evergreen. All grow best where winters are cold; once established, they are drought resistant. Pears grow best in full sun. Most are subject to fire blight. Listed below are ornamental, not fruiting, species.

Pyrus calleryana
Callery pear

Deciduous
Zones 5-9
Native to Eurasia and North Africa
Moderate growing to 25-50 feet tall and 15-20 feet wide; form varies by cultivar from broad-based oval to conical

If any one tree illustrates what can be done through selection, it's the callery pear. The species has many good qualities: abundant, early spring bloom; brilliant crimson-red fall color; shiny, dark green leaves with scalloped edges; and significant adaptability. It has three basic problems, however: thorns, susceptibility to fire blight, and messy, inedible fruits.

With the development of cultivars that are thornless and fire-blight resistant, and that have small fruit of only minor inconvenience, this tree has become an attractive and versatile specimen. The cultivars are generally highly adaptable and can tolerate urban pollution, high winds, and stressful conditions. They are undemanding as to soil type,

are drought resistant, require little maintenance, and are relatively pest free.

The cultivar 'Bradford' grows to 50 feet by 30 feet, has an oval shape and spreading, upright branches. It is thornless, usually fruitless, and has spectacular fall color. Because of its numerous attributes, this cultivar has been greatly overplanted. With age it becomes very brittle and is now banned in many communities.

'Chanticleer' has a narrower, pyramidal shape.

'Aristocrat' is pyramidal with wide-spaced, horizontal branches. It also has a glossier leaf with wavier edges.

'Faureri', sometimes available, is a 20-foot dwarf form with an oval habit, known primarily for its profuse flower show. Its branches are thought to be stronger than those of 'Bradford'.

Pyrus kawakamii
Evergreen pear

Evergreen
Zones 8-10
Native to Taiwan

Moderate growing to 30 feet; open, irregular habit

Evergreen pear is one of the most widely used trees in California. It grows naturally into a spreading shrub but is most commonly pruned into a single or multitrunked tree. The blossoms cover the tree from late winter through spring in a showy mass of white. The leaves are a shiny light green with wavy edges. This tree is adaptable to many soil types and needs minimum care; it is easy to espalier and good in containers near the patio or on the street.

Aphids and fire blight are two problems common to evergreen pear. Watch carefully for signs of fire blight; it can quickly destroy the beauty of the tree.

QUERCUS
OAK

Oaks are among the most valuable and important native trees in the United States. Since most of the larger species are long-lived, they are preferred landscape trees where space permits. They would be much

Quercus alba (white oak)

Quercus palustris (pin oak)

more heavily planted were it not that some are difficult to transplant and require more growing space than other trees.

Because oaks can reach such an impressive size and age, they are usually thought of as slow-growing trees. But this is not always true. In their native soil types, they are surprisingly fast growing. Oak species can be differentiated and identified by the size and shape of their acorns and the way the acorn "caps" are worn.

Oaks hybridize, and such hybrids are frequently the equal of or better than their parents. Still, propagation of these superior trees continues to be a challenge to growers.

Oak furniture and flooring are prized for their hard and long-lasting wood. Park land with a high percentage of oaks is highly desirable.

Quercus acutissima
Sawtooth oak

Deciduous
Zones 6–9
Native to Korea, China, and Japan

Moderate growing to 30–50 feet, upward-curving branches

This oak is not very common in the United States and Canada in spite of its good qualities. Its foliage is a deep, rich green that turns yellow in the fall. The gray-brown bark develops deep furrows with age.

Sawtooth oak responds well to full sun and rich, moist soil. It will grow in lesser soils, however, and is a good candidate for urban planting.

Quercus agrifolia
Coast live oak

Evergreen
Zone 9
Native to California
Slow growing to 20–70 feet with a rounded, wide-spreading head

Coast live oak has smooth, gray bark and a dense head and makes an excellent shade tree. It has shiny, hollylike leaves about 1 to 2½ inches long. It flowers in the early spring; fruits are acorns, maturing in one season.

Quercus alba
White oak

Deciduous
Zones 4–9
Native to the eastern United States
Moderate growing to 60–80 feet tall and equally wide

White oak has a pyramidal shape when young but matures slowly to a dense and broadly rounded tree. This imposing specimen has little trouble with pests or diseases but must have well-drained, acidic soil with plenty of moisture. These stately trees are very long-lived, sometimes 300 years or more under the right conditions.

Quercus coccinea
Scarlet oak

Deciduous
Zones 4–9
Native to the eastern and southern United States
Moderate to fast growing to 50–80 feet

This species is valued for its outstanding fall color. It thrives in full sun but does not do well in alkaline soils. It is also among the fastest-growing oaks and is relatively pest free.

Quercus macrocarpa
Bur oak

Deciduous
Zones 3–9
Native to Nova Scotia through Texas
Slow growing to 60–80 feet

The mature bur oak is impressive in winter with its pillar-like trunk and its sturdy, long, and twisting branches. Younger twigs are irregularly covered with corklike ridges, sometimes extending ½ inch or so above the diameter of the twig. This oak is drought tolerant and long-lived.

Quercus palustris
Pin oak

Deciduous
Zones 5–9
Native to the eastern United States
Fairly fast growing to 60–80 feet

Experts generally regard the pin oak as the easiest to transplant. This fact, plus its very

Quercus rubra (red oak)

Rhamnus alaternus (Italian buckthorn)

Rhus chinensis 'September Beauty'
(September Beauty Chinese sumac)

desirable form; glossy, fingered leaves; and generally good tolerance of a wide variety of planting sites, has made it the most popular native oak in the eastern United States.

The drooping habit of the lower branches makes this tree a poor choice where automobile or foot traffic must pass close by or underneath. This species is susceptible to iron chlorosis in alkaline soils.

Quercus phellos
Willow oak

Deciduous
Zones 6–9
Native to New York through Florida and to Texas
Rapid growing to 50–80 feet; round to conical when mature

Willow oak is the most graceful of all the oaks, with its slim, willowlike leaves that are 1 inch wide and 2 to 5 inches long. This tree takes full sun or light shade and well-drained soil. In southern areas it is partially evergreen, but the bright green leaves turn yellow to rust in cooler climates. In northern

areas, plants of northern origin should be used to ensure maximum winter hardiness.

Quercus robur
English oak

Deciduous
Zones 5–9
Native to Africa, Europe, and Asia
Moderate to fast growing to 80 feet with a wide head and a fairly short trunk

This long-lived oak becomes broad and spreading with maturity. It has little fall color and does not drop its leaves until late in the season. English oak is very susceptible to powdery mildew as autumn approaches. This is not a fatal condition, but it is unsightly (see page 39).

Quercus rubra
Red oak

Deciduous
Zones 5–9
Native to eastern North America
Fast growing to 60–80 feet

Red oak is second only to the scarlet oak in its fall color. It is adaptable, fast growing, fairly easy to transplant, and highly tolerant of urban conditions.

Rhamnus alaternus
Italian buckthorn

Evergreen
Zones 7–9
Native to southern Europe
Fast growing, tall shrub to 12–20 feet tall and equally wide

Italian buckthorn has small, shiny, green leaves and tiny spring flowers followed by berrylike black fruit. It is valued as a high screen or hedge and responds well to shearing. This tree can be trained to be either single stemmed or multitrunked.

RHUS
SUMAC

These deciduous shrubs or small trees range from 3 to 30 feet tall and spread as wide. Their velvety, dark red, spikelike seed heads and brilliant foliage are a part of the splendor of autumn across much of the

United States. Most are best used in natural settings or grouped on slopes. A few are of special ornamental value. Cutleaf forms make fine specimens. All do very well in dry soil of almost any kind and tolerate pollution. Most grow so quickly that they are weak wooded. Individual trunks may be relatively short-lived, but plants quickly rejuvenate from the base. Some sumacs have flowers of separate sexes on separate plants; male plants will never fruit. Sumacs grow best in full sun.

Rhus chinensis 'September Beauty'
September Beauty Chinese sumac

Deciduous
Zones 4–8
Cultivar of garden origin; species is native to China
Fast growing to 20 feet tall and equally wide

This cultivar is covered with big panicles of small white flowers in early September, when few other woody plants

Robinia pseudoacacia
(black locust)

Salix babylonica (weeping Babylon willow)

Salix matsudana (hankow willow)

are blooming. Its foliage is typical of sumac—lush and tropical looking, with compound leaves. 'September Beauty' does well in a hot, sunny site and is very stress tolerant. It does have a tendency to sucker, a trait that may require a bit of extra pruning.

Rhus lancea
African sumac

Evergreen
Zones 8–10
Native to South Africa
Slow growing to 25 feet tall and equally wide; open, spreading form

This graceful tree has a weeping appearance. Its foliage is green and willowlike. African sumac is widely adapted and is a good tree for desert locations because of its drought tolerance.

Robinia pseudoacacia
Black locust

Deciduous
Zones 4–9
Native to the east central United States

Fast growing to 40–75 feet tall and 30–60 feet wide; often multistemmed; umbrellalike in form with sparse, open branches

The young leaflets of black locust are silvery gray-green, turning dark green with age, and yellow in fall. Fragrant, pea-shaped flowers grow in long, pendant clusters and are attractive to bees. The flowers are followed by thin, flat brown pods that persist through the winter. The thorny bark is rough and deeply furrowed.

Black locust is a good choice for poor soils and otherwise difficult situations. It takes heat, drought, all types of soil, and neglect. This is a quick-growing tree, subject to several pests, most notably the locust borer. Its heavy thorns, invasive and suckering root system, and weak wood mean this otherwise attractive tree requires special consideration before planting. After it is cut down, eradicating suckering roots may take years.

SALIX
WILLOW

Where other choices are possible, willows are often frowned upon, as they have many drawbacks. The wood is brittle, it is impossible to garden around the roots, they have many pests, and they are constantly dropping leaves. However, their graceful, weeping habit is hard to match. Willows are beautiful, quick-growing trees, widely adapted to soil and climate, needing only abundant moisture.

Salix alba var. tristis
Golden weeping willow

Deciduous
Zones 2–9
Native to Europe, northern Africa, and Asia
Fast growing to 80 feet with greater spread; broad, open, round topped, low branching

This is one of the most beautiful varieties of weeping willow. The branches will eventually touch the ground unless the main stem is staked to 15 feet and the branches are kept well

pruned. The leaves are bright green to yellow-green with pale undersides.

Salix babylonica
Weeping Babylon willow

Deciduous
Zones 7–9
Native to China
Fast growing to 30–50 feet with a wider spread; heavy, round headed, with branchlets drooping to the ground

Weeping Babylon willow takes its name from its pronounced pendulous form. The long leaves are medium olive green, turning yellow in the fall. The branchlets are green to brown. This tree needs room to grow and may need training to develop a single trunk. It makes a good screen and an interesting winter silhouette.

Salix matsudana
Hankow willow

Deciduous
Zones 5–9
Native to northern Asia
Fast growing to 35–45 feet; pyramidal

Sapium sebiferum (Chinese tallow tree)

Sassafras albidum (sassafras)

Schinus molle (pepper tree)

Two cultivars are more common than the species. 'Tortuosa', corkscrew willow, is grown for its corkscrew branches, twisted leaves, and interesting winter character. 'Umbraculifera', globe willow, is a valuable plant in dry areas because of its drought tolerance. It forms a round-headed tree 35 to 40 feet high.

SAPIUM
TALLOW TREE

The members of this group of tropical and temperate deciduous shrubs and trees are native to China, Korea, Japan, and South America. They have poplarlike foliage; often an interesting, spreading, asymmetrical habit; and brilliant, long-lasting autumn color. They make fine shade or accent trees. Ornamental varieties are very insect and disease free and adaptable to many soils. They color best in full sun.

The Chinese use the waxy coating of sapium seeds to make candles and soap and for dressing cloth. The greasy sap of some species is poisonous. Some South American species

are good sources of rubber. Jumping beans are *Sapium* seeds containing insect grubs that cause the beans to jump.

Sapium japonicum
Japanese sapium

Deciduous
Zones 6–8
Native to China and Korea
Moderate growing to about 20 feet and rather upright

Japanese sapium has outstanding, brilliant, orange-red autumn color lasting for 10 days to 2 weeks. Flowers and fruit are small and interesting but not particularly showy.

This is an open-growing tree that is ideal for small gardens and patios. It is considered to be relatively pest free.

Sapium sebiferum
Chinese tallow tree

Deciduous
Zones 8–10
Native to China; naturalized in the southeastern United States
Fast growing to 40 feet tall and equally wide; round headed to conical

Despite its dense foliage, the Chinese tallow tree has an airy feel; it provides light shade throughout the summer. The leaves turn bronze to bright red after a sharp frost. Pruning in the early stages will confine this tree to a single trunk. A good lawn or street tree, it can also be used as a shade tree by a patio or on a terrace. It also makes a good screen.

This tree tolerates moist soils but prefers acid conditions. Ample water will encourage fast growth. The Chinese tallow tree is a good pest- and disease-free substitute for the poplar.

Sassafras albidum
Sassafras

Deciduous
Zones 5–9
Native to the eastern United States
Moderate growing to 30–50 feet; irregular habit

This tree is common to eastern hedgerows and woodlands but is difficult to transplant and therefore not often available.

It has interesting foliage and excellent yellow to red fall color. The leaves are bright green, and several leaf shapes may be found on the same branch. Leaves may have two lobes, a one-lobe mitten shape, or no lobes at all.

The flowers on female trees are followed by dark blue berries with bright red stalks that are quite attractive when viewed up close.

These trees are commonly bothered by Japanese beetles. They are native to acid soils and can be used effectively in woodland borders, parks, and other large areas.

Schinus molle
Pepper tree

Evergreen
Zones 9, 10
Native to Peru, Bolivia, and Chile
Fast growing to 20–50 feet; rounded, with wide-spreading, weeping branches

Although commonly called the pepper tree, this species is not a member of the true pepper family. It is a tree of beautiful

Sequoia sempervirens
(coast redwood)

Sequoiadendron giganteum (giant redwood)

Sophora japonica (Japanese pagoda tree, Chinese-scholar tree)

character and provides pleasant shade. Its leaves were once used to speed germination of seed corn. The Incas ground its red berries to produce an intoxicating beverage.

Schinus has a well-deserved reputation for growing rapidly with very little encouragement. It accepts poor soils, scant rainfall, strong winds, and occasional frost.

The shallow root system can lift pavement, and the tree is highly susceptible to aphids and black scale. Also, the fruits can become a litter problem.

Sequoia sempervirens
Coast redwood

Needled evergreen
Zones 7-9
Native to the coast ranges of Oregon and California
Fast growing to 50–70 feet in the garden; narrow, pyramidal form

Coast redwood is best adapted to the fog belt of northern California and Oregon, where it can receive year-round moisture. The attractiveness and fast-growing habit of this tree has prompted plantings out of

its native range throughout California. Selected forms eliminate the problem of seedling variability.

'Aptos Blue' has heavy, blue-green foliage.

'Santa Cruz' is a full, dense tree with soft-textured, light-green foliage.

'Los Altos' has glossy foliage and a rich green color that persists even in winter.

Sequoiadendron giganteum
Giant redwood

Needled evergreen
Zones 6-9
Native to the west slope of California's Sierra Nevada Mountains from Placer County to Tulare County, occurring in disconnected groves
Moderate growing to as high as 350 feet in natural stands, much less in the garden; pyramidal

There are few similarities between this tree and the coast redwood. The giant redwood is more distinctly pyramidal, and the foliage is denser, stiffer, and scalelike compared to the

soft, airy coast redwood. Also, the giant redwood doesn't require constant moisture and is hardier. The foliage is gray-green. This tree is best used in large, open areas.

Sophora japonica
Japanese pagoda tree,
Chinese-scholar tree

Deciduous
Zones 5-10
Native to China
Moderate growing to 50–70 feet, equally wide spread; dense, upright form when young, becoming round and spreading with age

The Japanese pagoda tree starts blooming when it is 8 to 10 years old. In bloom, it is covered with large, loose clusters of creamy white, pea-shaped blossoms for at least three weeks, longer in areas where summers are cool. These trees are extremely regular in their blooming habits. In a given geographic area, they all come into bloom almost on the same day no matter where they are growing—on streets, in gardens, or in parks.

The leaves are compound, and their fall color is yellow. They provide filtered shade.

Japanese pagoda trees require little pruning. Small branches on the inside of the tree will naturally die off. In a year or so they drop and the parent branch heals over. The branch dieback allows the wind to blow through these trees, so they do not usually suffer from wind or ice storm damage.

SORBUS
MOUNTAIN ASH

Mountain ashes are graceful, distinctive, deciduous trees with lovely, fragrant flowers and clusters of bright berries in the fall. Some have brilliant autumn color. They make excellent accent or shade trees alone, good screens or windbreaks when planted in mass. They are also used at the sunny edge of woodland plantings. Insects and diseases may be a problem in areas where summers are hot and dry. All mountain ashes need full sun and seem to do best in rich,

Sorbus aucuparia (European mountain ash)

Stewartia pseudocamellia (Japanese stewartia)

moist, but well-drained soil. Shape, foliage, and color of berries can vary with species, variety, or cultivar.

Sorbus alnifolia
Korean mountain ash

Deciduous
Zones 5–7
Native to central China, Korea, and Japan
Moderate growing to 25–35 feet; oval form

This tree has densely packed, shiny leaves. The leaves resemble those of certain crab apple trees and are not compound like those of other mountain ashes. The flowers are pure white, abundantly produced in small clusters, and followed by masses of bright scarlet berries in the fall. The fall foliage assumes brilliant shades of scarlet and crimson. This variety remains scarce, despite its great merits, because the seed is very difficult to germinate. It is highly resistant to trunk borers common to most other mountain ash species.

'Redbird' is even more showy than the wild species. It grows more erect and has fine, dark green leaves. It produces abundant fruit.

Sorbus aucuparia
European mountain ash

Deciduous
Zones 3–7
Native to Europe and Asia
Moderate growing to 25–30 feet; narrow, upright form rounding with maturity

This is the most commonly grown and most popular mountain ash species. Its enormous clusters of bright red berries are most showy when they color up in late summer and early fall. Its great enemies are trunk borers, which are more serious where summers are hot and dry. Fire blight is also a problem and makes it difficult to grow this tree in some areas.

Having been cultivated for so long, European mountain ash has given rise to many varieties, some with yellow berries, one with doubly cut leaves, and others with distinctive habits of growth.

Stenocarpus sinuatus
Firewheel tree

Evergreen
Zones 9, 10
Native to Queensland, Australia
Moderate growing to 15–20 feet tall and 10–15 feet wide

This excellent tree has very large, beautifully designed leaves that are rich, glossy green. After about five years, it will begin to produce the bizarre inflorescence that gives rise to its common name. Borne in fiery red clusters, the separate blooms have been likened to miniature crowns or pinwheels. The twelve or more radiating spokes are actually individual flowers so symmetrically arranged that the 2- to 3-inch wheel looks quite artificial. This tree prefers acidic soil and needs regular food and water. It does well in partial shade.

STEWARTIA
STEWARTIA

These choice accent trees are lovely the year around. Deciduous and slow growing, they bloom in early summer when few other trees do. They have good orange-red to purplish autumn color and interesting winter bark. They do best with morning sun and afternoon shade or in a woodland to prevent leaf scorch.

Stewartias are sometimes hard to find and are difficult to transplant. They should be moved only when small. These trees require partial shade and shelter from cold winds and do best in moist, acidic soil that is rich in humus and leaf mold.

Stewartia koreana
Korean stewartia

Deciduous
Zones 6–8
Native to Korea
Slow growing to 30–35 feet; pyramidal

The Korean stewartia is the hardiest of the various species

Styrax obassia (fragrant snowbell)

Syringa reticulata (S. amurensis var. *japonica)* (Japanese lilac tree)

and has the showiest flowers. Flowers are 3 inches across and white with golden centers—like single camellias. Starting in early June, they open successively for a three-week period. The bark of this tree has an interesting smooth, mottled appearance, and its foliage is a striking orange-red in the fall. This is a lovely and unusual tree and is attractive each season of the year. Some gardeners combine it with *S. pseudocamellia* (see next entry).

Stewartia pseudocamellia
Japanese stewartia

Deciduous
Zones 6–8
Native to Japan
Slow growing to 50–60 feet; pyramidal

Like Korean stewartia, this is an all-season performer. The bright green foliage is neat and attractive and turns shades of crimson and purple in the fall. Large white flowers with gold centers are borne in abundance over a long period in mid-summer. The attractive branch silhouette and beautiful red, flaking bark are especially prominent in winter.

STYRAX
SNOWBELL

These shrubs or small trees include both deciduous and evergreen species, but deciduous ones are more common. Snowbell is prized for its late-spring profusion of fragrant white flowers that hang below the leaves. Wide spreading, with rather dense, attractive, dark green foliage, these are excellent specimen trees for patio, lawn, or border. They are trouble free and grow with medium speed, blooming while quite young. Snowbell grows in sun or shade and does best in moist, well-drained, acidic soil.

Styrax japonicus
Japanese snowbell, Japanese snowdrop tree

Deciduous
Zones 5–8
Native to Japan, Korea, and China
Slow to moderate growing to about 15–20 feet; horizontal branching forms a spreading, flat-topped tree

Many observers consider this one of the best small garden trees. It is a neat, very bushy little tree with clean foliage and an attractive zigzag habit of branching. It is especially nice planted over a patio because the pendant flowers, which look like white fuchsia blossoms, are most handsome when viewed from below. They are borne in great abundance in early June. The whole tree looks white during its long blooming period.

Japanese snowbell tolerates shade and grows best in rich, well-drained soil. When young, it will need training to control shrubbiness.

Styrax obassia
Fragrant snowbell

Deciduous
Zones 5–8
Native to Japan and Korea
Moderate growing to 20–30 feet and about 12 feet wide

The dense, upright branches of this tree tend to hide its fragrant, 6- to 8-inch-long clusters of white flowers that bloom in midspring (somewhat earlier than the Japanese snowbell).

The leaves are large, 3 to 8 inches long, and oval. They are boldly textured, unlike Japanese snowbell foliage, which is fine in texture. This is an excellent patio plant and good in combination with azaleas, rhododendrons, and mountain laurel. It grows best in acidic soil and is usually trouble free. This species transplants best when young.

Syringa reticulata (S. amurensis var. japonica)
Japanese lilac tree

Deciduous
Zones 4–7
Native to Japan and Korea

Taxodium distichum (bald cypress)

Thuja occidentalis (American arborvitae, northern white cedar)

Moderate growing to 20–35 feet tall and about 15–25 feet wide; open, upright, spreading branches with round outline

This lovely little tree was popular in Victorian times but is less common today. It has large, pyramidal clusters of creamy white flowers, clean, disease-free foliage, and interesting cherrylike bark. The flowers have an unusual odor similar to the fragrance of privet. They appear in late spring or early summer, making this among the latest flowering lilacs. Japanese lilac tree is drought resistant and will thrive where dogwoods and other less tolerant flowering trees soon die out. It can be used as a small shade tree or as a street tree under utility wires.

Taxodium distichum

Bald cypress

Deciduous conifer
Zones 5–10
Native to Delaware through Florida and west into Texas
Moderate to fast growing to 50–100 feet

Bald cypress is tolerant of both drought and poor drainage. It has tiny leaves that do not need raking. In fact, the leaves are too small to rake. This conifer is deciduous and, therefore, good as a shade tree that will let in the winter sun. It has a rather slender shape that allows it to fit where space is somewhat limited and is an excellent tree for urban use.

Air is important to the roots of plants, and few woody plants can survive in aquatic situations. Those that can, such as this species, are usually well adapted to urban conditions, where soils are often poorly aerated.

THUJA
ARBORVITAE

These are fine, soft-leaved evergreens for accents, hedges, foundation plantings, or screens. All need full sun and will shed some foliage in the fall. The eastern and western arborvitaes need deep, moist

soil and high humidity; others will adapt to any average soil. Prune these trees to one central leader, and protect them from winter damage by lifting the snow off gently with a broom or by tying branches together so that the weight of snow and ice cannot bend them out of shape or break them off.

Arborvitae do best with some protection from winter winds and will grow in either acid or alkaline soil. A permanent mulch helps. No regular pruning is necessary.

Thuja occidentalis

American arborvitae, northern white cedar

Needled evergreen
Zones 3–9
Native to southeastern Canada and the northeastern United States
Slow to moderate growing to 40–50 feet tall; narrow, pyramidal

This tree displays bright green to yellow-green foliage in flat sprays on branches with upsweeping tips. In winter, it

turns an unattractive yellowish brown, except in certain selected cultivars.

American arborvitae will tolerate wet soil, but it can topple in the wind in open, wet areas. It is more stable on drier sites. This tree makes an effective hedge or tall screen. Columnar forms, commonly sold as 'Fastigiata', 'Columnaris', or 'Pyramidalis', are available. Other selections vary in height and foliage color.

Thuja plicata

Western red cedar, giant arborvitae, canoe cedar

Needled evergreen
Zones 5–8
Native to Alaska through northern California and across to Montana
Moderate growing to as high as 130–200 feet where native, usually much less in cultivation; pyramidal

This tree is a common sight in the northwestern United States. The foliage of the species is bright to dark green and lacy. The branches are slender.

Thuja plicata (western red cedar)

Tilia cordata (littleleaf linden)

Western red cedar tolerates wet soils but under such conditions the roots can pancake, that is, spread close to the surface rather than grow deep down in the ground. This makes the tree unstable in high winds when unprotected. Western red cedar takes shearing, is a valuable large hedge or screen tree, and looks good in large, open areas where its lower branches can sweep the ground. This is an excellent skyline tree in the Northwest. In the east it is smaller but greatly valued for its lush, evergreen foliage.

'Fastigiata' has an upright, columnar form and is an especially effective tall screen.

TILIA
LINDEN

The lindens are among the best large, deciduous shade or street trees. They are highly valued and often used in both the United States and Europe. Those native to Europe seem to be the most vigorous and handsome. Lindens are easily identified by their heart-shaped leaves that are unequal at the base. Their clusters of pendant, yellow flowers are small and somewhat inconspicuous but are quite fragrant. Some lindens may suffer insect damage but are rarely subject to lasting harm. Generally lindens grow slowly but reliably, doing especially well in full sun and moist soil.

Tilia cordata
Littleleaf linden

Deciduous
Zones 4–9
Native to Europe
Moderate to fast growing to 60–100 feet

This is a finely textured tree whose leaf has the dark green color and heart shape of a typical linden leaf but is smaller (1¼ to 2½ inches long, compared to the 3- to 5-inch leaf of most lindens). Its symmetrical habit has made it a very popular street, lawn, or shade tree. It can also be pollarded (see page 27) or trimmed into an effective hedge.

This tree can stand adverse city conditions, heat, and drought, although it grows best in moist, fertile, nonalkaline soil. It is, however, particularly susceptible to damage from de-icing salts.

Like other lindens, this species bears clusters of very fragrant yellow flowers in late spring or early summer.

Tilia tomentosa
Silver linden

Deciduous
Zones 4–7
Native from southeastern Europe to western Asia
Moderate to fast growing to 50–90 feet; spreads to about 35 feet at maturity

This is a striking specimen tree. From a distance its unique, dense, broad, pyramidal form appears sheared. Round to oval leaves are 2 to 4 inches long, gray-green on top, and covered with fine, short hairs on the undersides. When the wind blows this tree has a shimmery, silvery appearance. The flowers, which appear in mid-July, are small and in-conspicuous, dull white to yellowish, but very fragrant.

This species seems to be well adapted to urban situations and makes a stately avenue tree.

TSUGA
HEMLOCK

These are the most graceful of the needled evergreens and are used for specimen trees, hedges, windbreaks, or background plantings. All have small, pendant cones, are easy to transplant, and will thrive with shearing, though little regular pruning is needed if you choose to let them grow naturally.

Hemlocks do well in sun to partial shade in a cool and moist climate with some wind protection. Mulch helps retain soil moisture. They grow best in acid to neutral soil. This is one evergreen not suitable as an indoor Christmas tree, since it drops its needles very quickly after being cut. This is not the plant of the legendary poisonings.

Tsuga canadensis (Canadian eastern hemlock)

Ulmus americana (American elm)

Tsuga canadensis

Canadian eastern hemlock

Needled evergreen
Zones 3–7
Native to northeastern North
America
Moderate growing to 60–90
feet; pyramidal

Canadian hemlock has graceful, horizontal branches, drooping at the tips and bearing
dense, flat, deep-green sprays
of short needles. Because of its
small twigs and fine texture,
this tree is well adapted to
shearing and is easily trained
into a thick hedge. A Canadian
eastern hemlock hedge can be
maintained at a very slowly
increasing height for decades.

These trees thrive in cool,
moist loam and tolerate light
shade. They do not do well in
dry winds, drought, and pro-
longed heat.

Young hemlocks look best
in mass plantings. They do,
however, make outstanding
specimens with age, especially
in a lawn. Hemlock scale,
woolly adelgid, and spider
mites are problems in several
eastern states.

Tsuga caroliniana

Carolina hemlock

Needled evergreen
Zones 5–7
Native to the mountains of
Virginia through Georgia
Moderate growing to 50–70
feet; pyramidal

This fine hemlock does best in
an environment similar to that
of the Canadian eastern hemlock, but it is not quite as
hardy. It requires an acid soil
and is slightly more tolerant of
city pollution.

ULMUS
ELM

Elms have long been treasured
for their deep shade; vaselike
form; gray, furrowed bark; and
sawtooth leaves with golden
yellow autumn color. They
have, however, been terribly
devastated by disease. Do not
plant elms without full knowledge of the latest situation and
needed care. This can change
from year to year with new research, so check with the local
nursery or county agricultural

extension office. Elms need full
sun and deep, moist, well-
drained soil.

Ulmus americana

American elm

Deciduous
Zones 3–9
Native to the eastern
United States
Fast growing to 100 feet; vase-
shaped, spreading head

Due to the widespread scourge
of Dutch elm disease, the future of this tree is in doubt.
Dutch elm disease is caused by
a fungus. The leaves of the
infected trees turn yellow and
then wilt and die. The sapwood, the wood directly under
the bark, develops brown
streaks, and eventually the entire tree dies. Researchers are
actively studying the devastating Dutch elm disease in the
hope of saving existing trees
and breeding potentially
disease-resistant elms.

Japanese zelkova (*Zelkova
serrata*, page 107) can be used
as one substitute for the
American elm. It is quite similar and far less susceptible to
Dutch elm disease.

Ulmus parvifolia

Chinese elm, laceback elm

Deciduous
Zones 5–9
Native to China, Korea,
and Japan
Fast growing to 40–60 feet;
oval form

Chinese elm is a good urban
street tree that is very tolerant
of alkaline, poor, and compacted soil, and of heat and
drought. It has small, clustered
leaves that give it an open canopy. The leaves are dark green,
turning pale yellow to purple in
the fall. As winter approaches,
subtle red clusters of fruit appear and add interest to the
tree. The exfoliating bark, however, is this tree's best aesthetic feature. With age, the
tree sheds the circular plates of
its brown bark, revealing pale
yellow inner bark.

Vitex agnus-castus (chaste tree, hemp tree)

Ziziphus jujuba (Chinese jujube)

Chinese elm grows rapidly in good conditions. It is highly resistant to Dutch elm disease and the elm leaf beetle. The wood is relatively strong but still somewhat brittle. The leaves are small and easily shredded by a rotary mower. Seedlings are variable and superior cultivars are becoming available.

VITEX
CHASTE TREE

This deciduous tree, sometimes listed among shrubs, has 270 mostly tropical species. In late summer its fragrant, upright spires of small pink, purple, or white flowers bloom. It has aromatic, fine-textured gray foliage in a loose, open habit.

Chaste tree has an exotic look that contrasts well with other plantings. It is likely to die back or die out in wet, cold winters or in the northern part of its hardiness area, although it will usually send up new shoots and flower again the following summer. It does best in warmer regions in any good garden soil.

Vitex agnus-castus
Chaste tree, hemp tree

Evergreen
Zones 7–10
Native to southern Europe
Slow growing and shrubby in cold climates and faster growing in warm climates to 6–20 feet; broad and spreading

This tree is often multitrunked. The leaflets are dark green above and gray beneath. It flowers best with summer heat; showy lilac blue flowers bloom in late summer and early fall. This species is best grown in full sun. In hot climates, it makes a good shade tree when trained high.

Vitex lucens
New Zealand chaste tree, puriri

Evergreen
Zones 9, 10
Native to New Zealand
Slow to moderate growing to 40–60 feet; round, spreading

The foliage of the New Zealand chaste tree is particularly

handsome, with large, rich green compound leaves of ruffled 5-inch leaflets. The small, pink, bell-shaped flowers are followed by rose red, cherry-like, inedible fruit. The New Zealand chaste tree requires deep, rich soil.

Zelkova serrata
Japanese zelkova

Deciduous
Zones 5–9
Native to Japan and Korea
Moderate to fast growing to 50–60 feet tall and equally as wide; round headed or vase shaped

Japanese zelkova is often used as a substitute for its closest relative, the American elm. The foliage is similar to that of the elms; it turns shades of yellow or red in fall, the most common color being russet. With age, the gray bark takes on an attractive mottling. The branching habit of this tree varies; avoid forms with very narrow crotches, as they may become weak with age.

This tree is not completely immune to Dutch elm disease but is highly resistant. Wilt may be a problem with this species. Many cultivars are available.

Ziziphus jujuba
Chinese jujube

Deciduous
Zones 6–9
Native to southeastern Europe and China
Moderate growing to 15–25 feet; vase shaped

Chinese jujube is widely adapted and is especially valuable in the high and low desert, as it is able to stand alkaline or saline soils and drought. Its 1- to 2-inch-long glossy, green leaves are markedly veined. Small, yellow flowers are followed by a fall crop of fruit with the taste of a meaty apple. When dried and candied, they resemble dates. The gnarled, rather rough trunk and drooping thorned branches are picturesque in winter.

Climate Zone Map

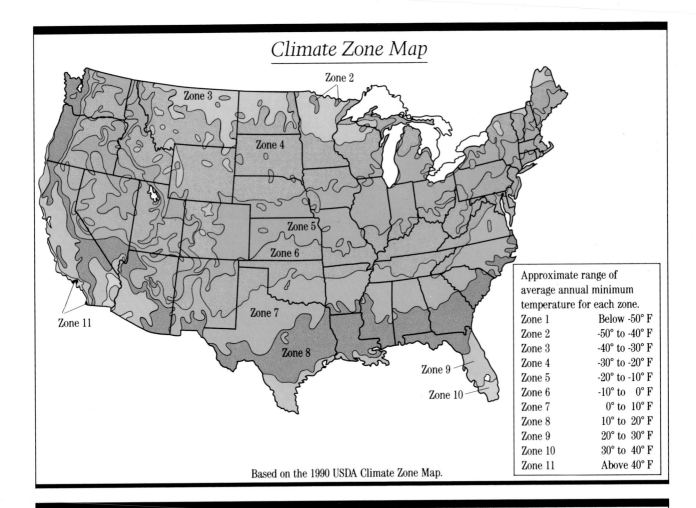

Approximate range of average annual minimum temperature for each zone.

Zone 1	Below -50° F
Zone 2	-50° to -40° F
Zone 3	-40° to -30° F
Zone 4	-30° to -20° F
Zone 5	-20° to -10° F
Zone 6	-10° to 0° F
Zone 7	0° to 10° F
Zone 8	10° to 20° F
Zone 9	20° to 30° F
Zone 10	30° to 40° F
Zone 11	Above 40° F

Based on the 1990 USDA Climate Zone Map.

U.S. Measure and Metric Measure Conversion Chart

	Symbol	When you know:	Multiply by:	To find:	Rounded Measures for Quick Reference		
Mass (Weight)	oz	ounces	28.35	grams	1 oz		= 30 g
	lb	pounds	0.45	kilograms	4 oz		= 115 g
	g	grams	0.035	ounces	8 oz		= 225 g
	kg	kilograms	2.2	pounds	16 oz	= 1 lb	= 450 g
					32 oz	= 2 lb	= 900 g
					36 oz	= 2¼ lb	= 1000g (1 kg)
Volume	pt	pints	0.47	liters	1 c	= 8 oz	= 250 ml
	qt	quarts	0.95	liters	2 c (1 pt)	= 16 oz	= 500 ml
	gal	gallons	3.785	liters	4 c (1 qt)	= 32 oz	= 1 liter
	ml	milliliters	0.034	fluid ounces	4 qt (1 gal)	= 128 oz	= 3¾ liter
Length	in.	inches	2.54	centimeters	⅜ in.	= 1 cm	
	ft	feet	30.48	centimeters	1 in.	= 2.5 cm	
	yd	yards	0.9144	meters	2 in.	= 5 cm	
	mi	miles	1.609	kilometers	2½ in.	= 6.5 cm	
	km	kilometers	0.621	miles	12 in. (1 ft)	= 30 cm	
	m	meters	1.094	yards	1 yd	= 90 cm	
	cm	centimeters	0.39	inches	100 ft	= 30 m	
					1 mi	= 1.6 km	
Temperature	° F	Fahrenheit	⅝ (after subtracting 32)	Celsius	32° F	= 0° C	
	° C	Celsius	⅝ (then add 32)	Fahrenheit	212° F	= 100° C	
Area	in.²	square inches	6.452	square centimeters	1 in.²	= 6.5 cm²	
	ft²	square feet	929.0	square centimeters	1 ft²	= 930 cm²	
	yd²	square yards	8361.0	square centimeters	1 yd²	= 8360 cm²	
	a.	acres	0.4047	hectares	1 a.	= 4050 m²	

Formulas for Exact Measures